About the book

"One's overall response to the book has to be 'Yes.' Yes, this describes a style of ministry desperately needed by all of us in the churches. Since we all minister to each other, the book is well recommended to those beyond the ranks of professional clergy. . . . Perhaps, just perhaps, prayerful reflection on this book will help many of us leave behind what was pompous and magical in the priesthood and enter into the mystery of Christian ministry, with the help of the first Wounded Healer."— *America*

". . . a lucid and profoundly simple book. . . . As a combination of creative case studies, stories from diverse cultures and religious traditions, perceptive cultural analysis, in-depth psychological and religious insights, and a balanced and creative theology, this small volume should prove exciting and intelligible for both clergy and laity."
—*The Christian Century*

"*The Wounded Healer* is Nouwen at his best. . . . For a short book, the ideas it implants linger long after the book is read, and re-read. It is realistic, hopeful and very, very personal. Highly recommended. . . ."—*Best Sellers*

". . . pervading [these] pages is a sense of spiritual depth. [It] is a book to give hope, renewed confidence and vision to the faltering will of the minister. Nouwen has stood in his shoes and speaks from a depth of insight and compassion."—*United Church Observer*

"What Father Nouwen has to say is real and challenging; straightforward, but not easy; basic, but by no means bookish."—*The Critic*

THE
WOUNDED HEALER

Other Books by Henri J.M. Nouwen

CLOWNING IN ROME

CREATIVE MINISTRY

A CRY FOR MERCY

REACHING OUT

THE GENESEE DIARY

THE WOUNDED HEALER

LIFESIGNS

THE ROAD TO DAYBREAK

THE
WOUNDED HEALER
Ministry in Contemporary Society

Henri J. M. Nouwen

TEXT COMPLETE AND UNABRIDGED

IMAGE BOOKS
DOUBLEDAY
NEW YORK   LONDON   TORONTO   SYDNEY   AUCKLAND

AN IMAGE BOOK
PUBLISHED BY DOUBLEDAY
a division of Bantam Doubleday Dell Publishing Group, Inc.
1540 Broadway, New York, New York 10036

IMAGE, DOUBLEDAY, and the portrayal of a deer drinking from
a stream are trademarks of Doubleday, a division of Bantam
Doubleday Dell Publishing Group, Inc.

First Image edition published March 1979 by special
arrangement with Doubleday, a division of Bantam Doubleday Dell
Publishing Group, Inc.

The chapter "Ministry for a Rootless Generation" first appeared
as "Generation Without Fathers" in *Commonweal* on June 12, 1970,
and is used here with grateful appreciation.

Library of Congress Cataloging-in-Publication Data
Nouwen, Henri J. M.
   The wounded healer: ministry in contemporary society/
   Henri J. M. Nouwen. —1st Image ed.
     p. cm.
   Reprint. Originally published: Doubleday. 1972.
   1. Pastoral theology. 2. Clergy—Office. 3. Pastoral
theology—Catholic Church. 4. Catholic Church—Clergy.
I. Title.
BV4011.N683   1990   89-29305
253—dc20   CIP

ISBN 0-385-14803-8

To Colin and Phyllis Williams

CONTENTS

ACKNOWLEDGMENTS

Many people have played an important role in the development of the different chapters of this book. Those to whom I presented parts of the manuscript in lecture form have been especially helpful in reorganizing and rephrasing major sections.

I am very grateful to Steve Thomas and Rufus Lusk for their substantial help in the final stage of the manuscript, to Inday Day for her excellent secretarial help, and to Elizabeth Bartelme for her encouragement and competent editorial assistance.

Many friends have made me aware, during the last year, of my male-dominated language. Going over the manuscript before publication, I realized how right they are. I hope that the women readers will have patience with my attempt for liberation, and will be able to recognize themselves even in the many "man's" and "he's". I hope to do better next time.

I have dedicated this book to Colin and Phyllis Williams, who by their friendship and hospitality made the Yale Divinity School a real free space for me.

INTRODUCTION

The Four Open Doors

What does it mean to be a minister in our contemporary society? This question has been raised during the last few years by many men and women who want to be of service, but who find the familiar ways crumbling and themselves stripped of their traditional protections.

The following chapters are an attempt to respond to this question. But as Antonio Porchia says: "A door opens to me. I go in and am faced with a hundred closed doors." (*Voices,* Chicago, 1969) Any new insight which suggested an answer led me to many new questions, which remained unanswered. But I wanted at least to prevent the temptation of not entering any doors at all out of fear of the closed ones. This explains the structure of this book. The four chapters can be seen as four different doors through which I have tried to enter into the problems of ministry in our modern world. The first door represents the condition of a suffering world (Chapter I); the second door, the condition of a suffering generation (Chapter 2); the third door, the condition of a suffering man (Chapter 3); and the fourth door, the condition of a suffering minister (Chapter 4). The unity of this book lies more in a tenacious attempt to respond to the ministers who are questioning their own relevance and effectiveness, than in a consistent theme, or a fully documented theoretical argument. Maybe our fragmented life experiences combined with our sense of urgency do not allow for a "handbook for ministers." However, in the middle of all fragmentation one image slowly arose as the focus of all considerations: the image of the wounded healer. This image was the last in coming. After all attempts to articulate the predicament of modern man, the necessity to articulate the predicament of the minister himself became most important. For the minister is called to recognize the sufferings of his time in his own heart and make that recognition the starting point of his service. Whether he tries to enter into a dislocated world, relate to a convulsive generation, or speak to a dying man, his service will not be perceived as authentic unless it comes from a heart wounded by the suffering about which he speaks.

Thus nothing can be written about ministry without a deeper understanding of the ways in which the minister can make his own wounds available as a source of healing. Therefore this book is called *The Wounded Healer*.

New Haven, Connecticut

THE
WOUNDED HEALER

CHAPTER I

MINISTRY IN A DISLOCATED WORLD

The Search of Nuclear Man

INTRODUCTION

From time to time a man enters into your life who, by his appearance, his behavior and his words, intimates in a dramatic way the condition of modern man. Such a man was Peter for me. He came to ask for help, but at the same time he offered a new understanding of my own world! Peter is twenty-six years old. His body is fragile; his face, framed in long blond hair, is thin with a city pallor. His eyes are tender and radiate a longing melancholy. His lips are sensual, and his smile evokes an atmosphere of intimacy. When he shakes hands he breaks through the formal ritual in such a way that you feel his body as really present. When he speaks, his voice assumes tones that ask to be listened to with careful attention.

As we talk, it becomes clear that Peter feels as if the many boundaries that give structure to life are becoming increasingly vague. His life seems a drifting over which he has no control, a life determined by many known and unknown factors in his surroundings. The clear distinction between himself and his milieu is gone and he feels that his ideas and feelings are not really his; rather, they are brought upon him. Sometimes he

3

wonders: "What is fantasy and what is reality?" Often he has the strange feeling that small devils enter his head and create a painful and anxious confusion. He also does not know whom he can trust and whom not, what he shall do and what not, why to say "yes" to one and "no" to another. The many distinctions between good and bad, ugly and beautiful, attractive and repulsive, are losing meaning for him. Even to the most bizarre suggestions he says: "Why not? Why not try something I have never tried? "Why not have a new experience, good or bad?"

In the absence of clear boundaries between himself and his milieu, between fantasy and reality, between what to do and what to avoid, it seems that Peter has become a prisoner of the now, caught in the present without meaningful connections with his past or future. When he goes home he feels that he enters a world which has become alien to him. The words his parents use, their questions and concerns, their aspirations and worries, seem to belong to another world, with another language and another mood. When he looks into his future everything becomes one big blur, an impenetrable cloud. He finds no answers to questions about why he lives and where he is heading. Peter is not working hard to reach a goal, he does not look forward to the fulfillment of a great desire, nor does he expect that something great or important is going to happen. He looks into empty space and is sure of only one thing: If there is anything worthwhile in life it must be here and now.

I did not paint this portrait of Peter to show you a picture of a sick man in need of psychiatric help. No, I think Peter's situation is in many ways typical of the condition of modern men and women. Perhaps Peter needs help, but his experiences and feelings cannot be understood merely in terms of individual psychopathology. They are part of the historical context in which we all live, a context which makes it possible to see in Peter's life the signs of the times, which we too recognize in our own life experiences. What we see in Peter is a painful expression of the situation of what I call "nuclear man."

In this chapter I would like to arrive at a deeper understanding of our human predicament as it becomes visible through the many men and women who experience life as Peter does. And I hope to discover in the midst of our present ferment new ways to liberation and freedom.

I will therefore divide this chapter into two parts: the predicament of nuclear man, and nuclear man's way to liberation.

I. THE PREDICAMENT OF NUCLEAR MAN

Nuclear man is a man who has lost naïve faith in the possibilities of technology and is painfully aware that the same powers that enable man to create new life styles carry the potential for self-destruction.

Let me tell you an old tale of ancient India which might help us to capture the situation of nuclear man:

> Four royal sons were questioning what specialty they should master. They said to one another, "Let us search the earth and learn a special science." So they decided, and after they had agreed on a place where they would meet again, the four brothers started off, each in a different direction.

5

Time went by, and the brothers met again at the appointed meeting place, and they asked one another what they had learned. "I have mastered a science," said the first, "which makes it possible for me, if I have nothing but a piece of bone of some creature, to create straightaway the flesh that goes with it." "I," said the second, "know how to grow that creature's skin and hair if there is flesh on its bones." The third said, "I am able to create its limbs if I have the flesh, the skin, and the hair." "And I," concluded the fourth, "know how to give life to that creature if its form is complete with limbs."

Thereupon the four brothers went into the jungle to find a piece of bone so that they could demonstrate their specialties. As fate would have it, the bone they found was a lion's, but they did not know that and picked up the bone. One added flesh to the bone, the second grew hide and hair, the third completed it with matching limbs, and the fourth gave the lion life. Shaking its heavy mane, the ferocious beast arose with its menacing mouth, sharp teeth, and merciless claws and jumped on his creators. He killed them all and vanished contentedly into the jungle.

From: *Tales of Ancient India,* translated from the Sanskrit by J. A. B. van Buitenen (New York: Bantam Books, 1961), pp. 50–51.

Nuclear man is the man who realizes that his creative powers hold the potential for self-destruction. He sees that in this nuclear age vast new industrial complexes enable man to produce in one hour that which he labored over for years in the past, but he also realizes that these same industries have disturbed the ecological balance and, through air and noise pollution, have contaminated his own milieu. He drives in cars, listens to the radio and watches TV, but has lost his ability to understand the workings of the instruments he uses. He sees such an abundance of material commodities around him that scarcity no longer motivates his life, but at the same time he is groping for a direction and asking for meaning and purpose. In all this he suffers from the inevitable knowledge that his time is a time in which it has become possible for man to destroy not only life but also the possibility of rebirth, not only man but also mankind, not only periods of existence but also history itself. For nuclear man the future has become an option.

The prenuclear man might be aware of the real paradox of a world in which life and death touch each other in a morbid way and in which man finds himself on the thin rope which can break so easily, but he has adapted this knowledge to his previous optimistic outlook on life. For nuclear man, however, this new knowledge cannot be adapted to old insights, nor be channeled by traditional institutions; rather it radically and definitively disrupts all existing frames of human reference. For him, the problem is not that the future holds a new danger, such as a nuclear war, but that there might be no future at all.

Young people are not necessarily nuclear, and old people are not necessarily prenuclear. The difference is not in age but in consciousness and the related life style. The psychohistorian Robert Jay Lifton has given us some excellent concepts to determine the nature of the quandaries of nuclear man. In Lifton's terms, nuclear man can be characterized by (1) a historical dislocation, (2) a fragmented ideology, and (3) a search for immortality. It might be useful to examine Peter's life in the light of these concepts.

1. Historical dislocation

When Peter's father asks him when he will take his final exam, and whether he has found a good girl to marry; and when his mother carefully inquires about confession and communion and his membership in a Catholic fraternity—they both suppose that Peter's expectations for the future are essentially the same as theirs. But Peter thinks of himself more as one of the "last ones in the experiment of living" than as a pioneer working for a new future. Therefore, symbols used by his parents cannot possibly have the unifying and integrating power for him which they have for people with a prenuclear mentality. This experience of Peter's we call "historical dislocation." It is a "break in the sense of connection, which men have long felt with the vital and nourishing symbol of their cultural tradition; symbols revolving around family, idea-systems, religion, and the life-cycle in general" (Lifton, *History and Human Survival,* New York: Random House, 1970, p. 318). Why should a man marry and have children, study and build a career; why should he invent new techniques, build new institutions, and develop new ideas—when he doubts if there will be a tomorrow which can guarantee the value of human effort?

Crucial here for nuclear man is the lack of a sense of continuity, which is so vital for a creative life. He finds himself part of a nonhistory in which only the sharp moment of the here and now is valuable. For nuclear man life easily becomes a bow whose string is broken

8

and from which no arrow can fly. In his dislocated state he becomes paralyzed. His reactions are not anxiety and joy, which were so much a part of existential man, but apathy and boredom. Only when man feels himself responsible for the future can he have hope or despair, but when he thinks of himself as the passive victim of an extremely complex technological bureaucracy, his motivation falters and he starts drifting from one moment to the next, making life a long row of randomly chained incidents and accidents.

When we wonder why the language of traditional Christianity has lost its liberating power for nuclear man, we have to realize that most Christian preaching is still based on the presupposition that man sees himself as meaningfully integrated with a history in which God came to us in the past, is living under us in the present, and will come to liberate us in the future. But when man's historical consciousness is broken, the whole Christian message seems like a lecture about the great pioneers to a boy on an acid trip.

2. Fragmented ideology

One of the most surprising aspects of Peter's life is his fast-shifting value system. For many years he was a very strict and obedient seminarian. He went to daily Mass, took part in the many hours of community prayers, was active in a liturgical committee, and studied with great interest and even enthusiasm the many theological materials for his courses. But when he decided to leave the seminary and study at a secular university, it took him only a few months to shake off his old way of life. He quietly stopped going to Mass even on Sundays, spent long nights drinking and playing with other students, lived with a girl friend, took up a field of study far removed from his theological interests, and seldom spoke about God or religion.

This is the more surprising since Peter shows absolutely no bitterness toward the old seminary. He even visits his friends there regularly and has good memories of his years as a religious man. But the idea that his two life styles are not very consistent hardly seems to hit him. Both experiences are valuable and have their good and bad sides, but why should life be lived in just one perspective, under the guidance of just one idea, and within one unchangeable frame of reference?

Peter does not regret his seminary days nor glorify his present situation. Tomorrow it might be different again. Who knows? All depends on the people you meet, the experiences you have, and the ideas and desires which make sense to you at the moment.

Nuclear man, like Peter, does not live with an ideology. He has shifted from the fixed and total forms of an ideology to more fluid ideological fragments (Lifton, *Boundaries,* New York: Random House, 1970, p. 98). One of the most visible phenomena of our time is the tremendous exposure of man to divergent and often contrasting ideas, traditions, religious convictions, and life styles. Through mass media he is confronted with the most paradoxical human experiences. He is confronted not only with the most elaborate and expensive attempts to save the life of one man by heart transplantation, but also with the powerlessness of the world to help when thousands of people die from lack of food. He is confronted not only with man's ability to travel rapidly to another planet, but also with his hopeless impotence to end a senseless war on this planet. He is confronted not only with high-level discussions about human rights and Christian morality, but also with torture chambers in Brazil,

10

Greece, and Vietnam. He is confronted not only with incredible ingenuity that can build dams, change river-beds and create fertile new lands, but also with earth-quakes, floods and tornadoes that can ruin in one hour more than man can build in a generation. A man confronted with all this and trying to make sense of it cannot possibly deceive himself with one idea, concept, or thought system which could bring these contrasting images together into one consistent outlook on life.

"The extraordinary flow of post-modern cultural influences" (Lifton, *History and Human Survival*, p. 318) asks a growing flexibility of the nuclear man, a willingness to remain open and live with the small fragments which at the moment seem to offer the best response to a given situation. Paradoxically, this can lead to moments of great exhilaration and exaltation in which man immerses himself totally in the flashing impressions of his immediate surroundings.

Nuclear man no longer believes in anything that is always and everywhere true and valid. He lives by the hour and creates his life on the spot. His art is a collage art, an art which, though a combination of divergent pieces, is a short impression of how man feels at the moment. His music is an improvisation which combines themes from various composers into something fresh as well as momentary. His life often looks like a playful expression of feelings and ideas that need to be communicated and reponded to, but which do not attempt to oblige anyone else.

This fragmented ideology can prevent nuclear man from becoming a fanatic who is willing to die or to kill for an idea. He is primarily looking for experiences that give him a sense of value. Therefore he is very tolerant, since he does not regard a man with a different conviction as a threat but rather as an opportunity to discover new ideas and test his own. He might listen with great attention to a rabbi, a minister, a priest, without considering the acceptance of any system of thought, but quite willing to deepen his own understanding of what he experiences as partial and fragmentary.

When nuclear man feels himself unable to relate to the Christian message, we may wonder whether this is not due to the fact that, for many people, Christianity has become an ideology. Jesus, a Jew executed by the leaders of his time, is quite often transformed into a cultural hero reinforcing the most divergent and often destructive ideological points of view. When Christianity is reduced to an all-encompassing ideology, nuclear man is all too prone to be skeptical about its relevance to his life experience.

3. A search for new immortality

Why did Peter come for help? He himself did not know exactly what he was looking for, but he had a general, all-pervading feeling of confusion. He had lost unity and direction in his life. He had lost the boundaries which could keep him together, and he felt like a prisoner of the present, drifting from left to right, unable to decide on a definitive course. He kept studying with a sort of obedient routine to give himself the feeling of having something to do, but the long weekends and many holidays were mostly spent in sleeping, lovemaking, and just sitting around with his friends, gently distracted by music and the free-floating images of his fantasy.

Nothing seemed urgent or even important enough to become involved in. No projects or plans, no exciting goals to work for, no pressing tasks to fulfill. Peter was not torn apart by conflict, was not depressed, suicidal, or anxiety-ridden. He did not suffer from despair, but neither did he have anything to hope for. This paralysis made him suspicious about his own condition. He had discovered that even the satisfaction of his desire to embrace, to kiss and to hold in a surrendering act of love, had not created the freedom to move and to take new steps forward. He started to wonder whether love really is enough to keep a man alive in this world, and whether, to be creative, man does not need to find a way to transcend the limitations of being human.

Perhaps we can find in Peter's life history events or experiences that throw some light on his apathy, but it seems just as valid to view Peter's paralysis as the paralysis of nuclear man who has lost the source of his creativity, which is his sense of immortality. When man is no longer able to look beyond his own death and relate himself to what extends beyond the time and space of his life, he loses his desire to create and the excitement of being human. Therefore, I want to look at Peter's problem as that of nuclear man who is searching for new ways of being immortal.

Robert Lifton sees as the core problem of man in the nuclear age the threat to his sense of immortality. This sense of immortality "represents a compelling, universal urge to maintain an inner sense of continuity over time and space, with the various elements of life." It is "man's way of experiencing his connection with all human history" (Lifton, *Boundaries,* p. 22). But for nuclear man the traditional modes of immortality have lost their connective power. Often he says: "I do not want to bring children into this self-destructive world." This means that the desire to live on in his children is

13

extinguished in the face of the possible end of history. And why should he want to live on in the works of his hands when one atomic blitz may reduce them to ashes in a second? Could perhaps an animistic immortality make it possible for man to live on in nature? And how can a belief in a "hereafter" be an answer to the search for immortality when there is hardly any belief in the "here"? A life after death can only be thought of in terms of life before it, and nobody can dream of a new earth when there is no old earth to hold any promises.

No form of immortality—neither the immortality through children nor the immortality through works, neither the immortality through nature nor the immortality in heaven—is able to help nuclear man project himself beyond the limitations of his human existence.

It is therefore certainly not surprising that nuclear man cannot find an adequate expression of his experience in symbols such as Hell, Purgatory, Heaven, Hereafter, Resurrection, Paradise, and the Kingdom of God.

A preaching and teaching still based on the assumption that man is on his way to a new land filled with promises, and that his creative activities in this world are the first signs of what he will see in the hereafter, cannot find a sounding board in a man whose mind is brooding on the suicidal potentials of his own world.

This brings us to the end of our description of nuclear man. Peter was our model. We saw his historical dislocation, his fragmented ideology, and his search for a new mode of immortality. Obviously, the level of awareness and visibility is different in different people, but I hope you will be able to recognize in your own experiences and the experiences of your friends some of the traits which are so visible in Peter's life style. And this recognition might also help you to realize that Christianity is not just challenged to adapt itself to a modern age, but is also challenged to ask itself whether its unarticulated suppositions can still form the basis for its redemptive pretensions.

II. NUCLEAR MAN'S WAY TO LIBERATION

When you recognize nuclear man among your colleagues, friends, and family, and maybe even in your own self-reflections, you cannot avoid asking if there is not a way to liberation and freedom for this new type of man. More important than constructing untested answers which tend to create more irritation than comfort, we might be able to uncover, in the midst of the present confusion and stagnation, new trails that point in hopeful directions.

When we look around us we see man paralyzed by dislocation and fragmentation, caught in the prison of his own mortality. However, we also see exhilarating experiments of living by which he tries to free himself of the chains of his own predicament, transcend his mortal condition, reach beyond himself, and experience the source of a new creativity.

My own involvement in the spasms and pains of nuclear man makes me suspect that there are two main ways by whch he tries to break out of his cocoon and fly: the mystical way and the revolutionary way. Both ways can be considered modes of "experiential transcendence" (Lifton, *History and Human Survival,* p. 330), and both ways seem to open new perspectives

15

and suggest new life styles. Let me therefore try to describe these two ways, and then show how they are interrelated.

1. *The mystical way*

The mystical way is the inner way. Man tries to find in his inner life a connection with the "reality of the unseen," "the source of being," "the point of silence." There he discovers that what is most personal is most universal (cf. Rogers' *On Becoming a Person*. Houghton Mifflin, 1961, p. 26). Beyond the superficial layers of idiosyncrasies, psychological differences and characterological typologies, he finds a center from which he can embrace all other beings at once and experience meaningful connections with all that exists. Many people who have made risky trips on LSD and returned safely from them, have spoken about sensations during which they temporarily broke through their alienation, felt an intimate closeness to the mysterious power that brings men together, and came to a liberating insight into what lies beyond death. The increasing number of houses for meditation, concentration, and contemplation, and the many new Zen and Yoga centers show that nuclear man is trying to reach a moment, a point or a center, in which the distinction between life and death can be transcended and in which a deep connection with all of nature, as well as with all of history, can be experienced. In whatever way we try to define this mode of "experiential transcendence," it seems that in all its forms man tries to transcend his own worldly environment and move one, two, three or more levels away from the unreali-

16

ties of his daily existence to a more encompassing view which enables him to experience what is real. In this experience he can cut through his apathy and reach the deep currents of life in which he participates. There he feels that he belongs to a story of which he knows neither the beginning nor the end, but in which he has a unique place. By this creative distance from the unrealities of his own ambitions and urges, nuclear man breaks through the vicious circle of the self-fulfilling prophecy that makes him suffer from his own morbid predictions. There he comes into contact with the center of his own creativity and finds the strength to refuse to become the passive victim of his own futurology. There he experiences himself no longer as an isolated individual caught in the diabolic chain of cause and effect, but as a man able to transcend the fences of his own predicament and reach out far beyond the concerns of self. There he touches the place where all people are revealed to him as equal and where compassion becomes a human possibility. There he comes to the shocking, but at the same time self-evident, insight that prayer is not a pious decoration of life but the breath of human existence.

2. *The revolutionary way*

But there is a second way which is becoming visible in the present-day world of nuclear man. It is the revolutionary way of transcending our human predicament. Here man becomes aware that the choice is no longer between his world or a better world, but between no world or a new world. It is the way of the man who says: Revolution is better than suicide. This man is deeply convinced that our world is heading for the edge of the cliff, that Auschwitz, Hiroshima, Algeria, Biafra, My Lai, Attica, Bangladesh, and Northern Ireland are only a few of the many names that show how man kills himself with his own absurd technological inventions. For him no adaptation, restoration or addition can help any longer. For him the liberals and progressives are fooling themselves by trying to make an intolerable situation a little more tolerable. He is tired of pruning trees and clipping branches; he wants to pull out the roots of a sick society. He no longer believes that integration talks, corporate measures against air and noise pollution, peace corps, antipoverty programs and civil-rights legislation will save a world dominated by extortion, oppression, and exploitation. Only a total radical upheaval of the existing order, together with a drastic change of direction, can prevent the end of everything. But while aiming at a revolution, he is not just motivated by a desire to liberate the oppressed, alleviate the poor, and end war. While in the past scarcity led man to revolt, the present-day revolutionary sees the urgent and immediate needs of his suffering fellow man as part of a much greater apocalyptic scene in which the survival of humanity itself is at stake. His goal is not a better man, but a new man, a man who relates to himself and his world in ways which are still unexplored but which belong to his hidden potentials. The life of this man is not ruled by manipulation and supported by weapons, but is ruled by love and supported by new ways of interpersonal communication. This new man, however, does not develop from a self-guiding process of evolution. He might or might not come about. Perhaps it is already too late. Perhaps the suicidal tendencies, visible in the

18

growing imbalance in culture as well as nature, have reached the point of no return. Still, the revolutionary believes that the situation is not irreversible and that a total reorientation of mankind is just as possible as is a total self-destruction. He does not think his goal will be reached in a few years or even in a few generations, but he bases his commitment on the conviction that it is better to give your life than to take it, and that the value of your actions does not depend on their immediate results. He lives by the vision of a new world and refuses to be sidetracked by trivial ambitions of the moment. Thus he transcends his present condition and moves from a passive fatalism to a radical activism.

3. The Christian way

Is there a third way, a Christian way? It is my growing conviction that in Jesus the mystical and the revolutionary ways are not opposites, but two sides of the same human mode of experiential transcendence. I am increasingly convinced that conversion is the individual equivalent of revolution. Therefore every real revolutionary is challenged to be a mystic at heart, and he who walks the mystical way is called to unmask the illusory quality of human society. Mysticism and revolution are two aspects of the same attempt to bring about radical change. No mystic can prevent himself from becoming a social critic, since in self-reflection he will discover the roots of a sick society. Similarly, no revolutionary can avoid facing his own human condition, since in the midst of his struggle for a new world he will find that he is also fighting his own reactionary fears and false ambitions.

The mystic as well as the revolutionary has to cut

loose from his selfish needs for a safe and protected existence and has to face without fear the miserable condition of himself and his world. It is certainly not surprising that the great revolutionary leaders and the great contemplatives of our time meet in their common concern to liberate nuclear man from his paralysis. Their personalities might be quite different, but they show the same vision, which leads to a radical self-criticism as well as to a radical activism. This vision is able to restore the "broken connection" (Lifton) with past and future, bring unity to a fragmented ideology, and reach beyond the limits of the mortal self. This vision can offer a creative distance from ourselves and our world and help us transcend the limiting walls of our human predicament.

For the mystic as well as for the revolutionary, life means breaking through the veil covering our human existence and following the vision that has become manifest to us. Whatever we call this vision—"The Holy," "The Numinon," "The Spirit," or "Father"—we still believe that conversion and revolution alike derive their power from a source beyond the limitations of our own createdness.

For a Christian, Jesus is the man in whom it has indeed become manifest that revolution and conversion cannot be separated in man's search for experiential transcendence. His appearance in our midst has made it undeniably clear that changing the human heart and changing human society are not separate tasks, but are as interconnected as the two beams of the cross.

Jesus was a revolutionary, who did not become an extremist, since he did not offer an ideology, but Himself. He was also a mystic, who did not use his intimate relationship with God to avoid the social evils of his time, but shocked his milieu to the point of being executed as a rebel. In this sense he also remains for nuclear man the way to liberation and freedom.

CONCLUSION

We saw the predicament of nuclear man, characterized by historical dislocation, fragmented ideology and the search for immortality. We discovered the mystical as well as the revolutionary way by which nuclear man tries to reach beyond himself. And finally we saw that for a Christian, the man Jesus had made it manifest that these two ways do not constitute a contradiction but are in fact two sides of the same mode of experiential transcendence.

I suppose you will hesitate to consider yourself a mystic or a revolutionary, but when you have eyes to see and ears to hear you will recognize him in your midst. He is sometimes undeniably evident to the point of irritation, sometimes only partially visible. You will find him in the eyes of the guerrilla, the young radical or the boy with the picket sign. You will notice him in the quiet dreamer playing his guitar in the corner of a coffeehouse, in the soft voice of a friendly monk, in the melancholic smile of a student concentrating on his reading. You will see him in the mother who allows her son to go his own difficult way, in the father who reads to his child from a strange book, in the loud laughter of a young girl, in the indignation of a Young Lord, and in the determination of a Black Panther.

You will find him in your own town, in your own family, and even in the strivings of your own heart, because he is in every man who draws his strength from

21

the vision that dawns on the skyline of his life and leads him to a new world.

It is this new world that fills our dreams, guides our actions and makes us go on, at great risk, with the increasing conviction that one day man will finally be free—free to love!

CHAPTER II

MINISTRY FOR A
ROOTLESS GENERATION

Looking into the Fugitive's Eyes

INTRODUCTION

To set the right tone for a discussion of Christian ministry in tomorrow's world, I like to start with a short tale.

One day a young fugitive, trying to hide himself from the enemy, entered a small village. The people were kind to him and offered him a place to stay. But when the soldiers who sought the fugitive asked where he was hiding, everyone became very fearful. The soldiers threatened to burn the village and kill every man in it unless the young man were handed over to them before dawn. The people went to the minister and asked him what to do. The minister, torn between handing over the boy to the enemy or having his people killed, withdrew to his room and read his Bible, hoping to find an answer before dawn. After many hours, in the early morning his eyes fell on these words: "It is better that one man dies than that the whole people be lost."

Then the minister closed the Bible, called the soldiers and told them where the boy was hidden. And after the soldiers led the fugitive away to be killed, there was a feast in the village because the minister had saved the lives of the people. But the minister did not celebrate. Overcome with a deep sadness, he remained in his room. That night an angel came to him, and asked, "What have you done?" He said: "I handed over the fugitive to the enemy." Then the angel said: "But don't you know that you have handed over the Messiah?" "How could I know?" the minister replied anxiously. Then the angel said: "If, instead of reading your Bible, you had visited this young man just once and looked into his eyes, you would have known."

While versions of this story are very old, it seems the most modern of tales. Like that minister, who might have recognized the Messiah if he had raised his eyes from his Bible to look into the youth's eyes, we are challenged to look into the eyes of the young men and women of today, who are running away from our cruel ways. Perhaps that will be enough to prevent us from handing them over to the enemy and enable us to lead them out of their hidden places into the middle of their people where they can redeem us from our fears.

It would seem, then, that we are faced with two questions. First, how do the men and women of tomorrow look today? And second, how can we lead them to where they can redeem their people?

I. THE MEN AND WOMEN OF TOMORROW

If the men and women of today are often thought of as anonymous members of Riesman's lonely crowd, the men and women of tomorrow will be the children of this lonely crowd. When we look into the eyes of young people, we can catch a glimpse of at least a shadow of their world. Christian leadership will be

26

shaped by at least three of the characteristics which the men and women of tomorrow share: inwardness, fatherlessness, and convulsiveness. The minister of tomorrow must indeed take a serious look at those characteristics in his reflections and planning.

We might therefore term this generation the inward generation, the generation without fathers, and the convulsive generation. Let us see how these characteristics help us to understand more fully the men and women of tomorrow.

1. The inward generation

In a recent study of today's college generation, published in October 1969, Jeffrey K. Hadden suggests that the best phrase with which to characterize the coming generation is "the inward generation." It is the generation which gives absolute priority to the personal and which tends in a remarkable way to withdraw into the self. This might surprise those who think of our youth as highly activist, sign-carrying protesters who stage teach-ins, sit-ins, walk-ins, and stay-ins all over the country and think of themselves in many terms, but never in terms of inwardness.

First impressions, however, are not always the right ones. Let me describe a recent development in a famous youth center in Amsterdam. Recently this center, called Fantasio, attracted thousands of young people from all over the world to its psychedelic, dreamlike atmosphere.

Fantasio was divided into many small, cozy, psychedelically painted rooms. Young people with long beards and long hair, in colorful clothing pieced together from old liturgical vestments, were sitting there quietly smoking their sticks, smelling their incense, enthralled by the flesh-and-blood pervading rock rhythms.

But now things are different. The young leaders have thrown out all psychedelic stimuli, remodeled their center into a very sober and more or less severe place, and have changed the center's name from Fantasio to: Meditation Center the Kosmos. In the first issue of their newspaper they wrote: "Cut off your long hair, throw away your beards, put on simple clothes, because now things are going to be serious." Concentration, contemplation, and meditation have become the key words of the place. Yogis give classes in body control, people sit and talk for many hours about Chuang Tzu and the Eastern mystics, and everyone is basically trying to find the road that leads inward.

We might be inclined to dismiss this group's behavior as the sort of peripheral oddity found in every modern society. But Jeffrey Hadden shows that this behavior is a symptom of something much more general, much more basic and much more influential. It is the behavior of people who are convinced that there is nothing "out there" or "up there" on which they can get a solid grasp, which can pull them out of their uncertainty and confusion. No authority, no institution, no outer concrete reality has the power to relieve them of their anxiety and loneliness and make them free. Therefore the only way is the inward way. If there is nothing "out there" or "up there," perhaps there is something meaningful, something solid "in there." Perhaps something deep in the most personal self holds the key to the mystery of meaning, freedom and unity.

The German sociologist Shelsky speaks about our time as a time of continuing reflection. Instead of an obvious authority telling us how to think and what to

28

do, this continuing reflection has entered into the center of our existence. Dogmas are the hidden realities men have to discover in their inner consciousness as sources of self-understanding. The modern mind, Shelsky says, is in a state of constant self-reflection, trying to penetrate deeper and deeper into the core of its own individuality.

But where does this lead us? What kind of men will this inward-moving, self-reflecting generation produce? Jeffrey K. Hadden writes:

> The prospects are both ominous and promising. If turning inward to discover the self is but a step toward becoming a sensitive and honest person, our society's unfettered faith in youth may turn out to be justified. However, inwardness' present mood and form seems unbridled by any social norm or tradition and almost void of notions for exercise of responsibility toward others. (*Psychology Today,* October 1969)

Jeffrey K. Hadden is the last one to suggest that the inward generation is on the brink of revitalizing the contemplative life, about to initiate new forms of monasticism. His data show, first of all, that inwardness can lead to a form of privatism, which is not only antiauthoritarian and anti-institutional, but is also very self-centered, highly interested in material comfort and the immediate gratification of existing needs and desires. But inwardness need not lead to such privatism. It is possible that the new reality discovered in the deepest self can be "molded into a commitment to transform society." The inwardness of the coming generation can lead either to a higher level of hypocrisy or to the discovery of the reality of the unseen which can

29

make for a new world. The path it takes will depend to a great extent on the kind of ministry given to this inward generation.

2. Generation without fathers

The many who call themselves father or allow themselves to be called father, from the Holy Father to the many father abbots, to the thousands of "priest-fathers" trying to hand over some good news, should know that the last one to be listened to is the father. We are facing a generation which has parents but no fathers, a generation in which everyone who claims authority—because he is older, more mature, more intelligent or more powerful—is suspect from the very beginning.

There was a time, and in many ways we see the last spastic movements of this time still around us, when man's identity, his manhood and power, were given him by the father from above. I am good when I am patted on the shoulder by him who stands above me. I am smart when some father gives me a good grade. I am important when I study at a well-known university as the intellectual child of a well-known professor. In short, I am whom I am considered to be by one of my many fathers.

We could have predicted that the coming generation would reject this, since we have already accepted that a man's worth is not dependent on what is given to him by fathers, but by what he makes of himself. We could have expected this, since we have said that faith is not the acceptance of centuries-old traditions but an attitude which grows from within. We could have anticipated this ever since we started saying that man is free to choose his own future, his own work, his own wife.

Today, seeing that the whole adult, fatherly world stands helpless before the threat of atomic war, eroding poverty, and starvation of millions, the men and women of tomorrow see that no father has anything to tell them simply because he has lived longer. An English beat group yells it out:

> The wall on which the prophets wrote
> Is cracking at the seams.
> Upon the instrument of death
> The sunlight brightly gleams.
> When ev'ry man is torn apart
> With nightmares and with dreams
> Will no one lay the laurel wreath
> As silence drowns the screams.*

This is what the coming generation is watching, and they know they can expect nothing from above. Looking into the adult world they say:

> I'm on the outside looking inside.
> What do I see?
> Much confusion disillusion all around me.
> You don't possess me
> Don't impress me
> Just upset my mind.
> Can't instruct me
> or conduct me
> Just use up my time.†

* Portions of the lyrics from "Epitaph." Words and music by Robert Fripp, Ian McDonald, Greg Lake, Michael Giles and Peter Sinfield. © Copyright 1969 and 1971 Enthoven Gaydon & Co., London, England. TRO-TOTAL MUSIC, INC., New York. Used by permission.

† Portion of the lyrics from "I Talk to the Wind." Words and music by Ian McDonald and Peter Sinfield. © Copyright 1969 Enthoven Gaydon & Co., London, England. TRO-TOTAL MUSIC, INC., New York. Used by permission.

The only thing left is to try it alone, not proud or contemptuous of the fathers, telling them that they will do better, but with the deep-seated fear of complete failure. But they prefer failure to believing in those who have already failed right before their eyes. They recognize themselves in the words of a modern song:

> Confusion will be my epitaph
> As I crawl a cracked and broken path.
> If we make it we can all sit back and laugh.
> But I fear tomorrow I'll be crying,
> Yes, I fear tomorrow I'll be crying.‡

But this fearful generation which rejects its fathers and quite often rejects the legitimacy of every person or institution that claims authority, is facing a new danger: becoming captive to itself. David Riesman says: "As adult authority disintegrates, the young are more and more the captives of each other. . . . When adult control disappears, the young's control of each other intensifies." (*Psychology Today,* October 1969) Instead of the father, the peer becomes the standard. Many young people who are completely unimpressed by the demands, expectations and complaints of the big bosses of the adult world, show a scrupulous sensitivity to what their peers feel, think and say about them. Being considered an outcast or a dropout by adults does not worry them. But being excommunicated by the small circle of friends to which they want to belong can be an unbearable experience. Many young people may even become enslaved by the tyranny of their peers. While appearing indifferent, casual and even

‡ Portions of the lyrics from "Epitaph." Words and music by Robert Fripp, Ian McDonald, Greg Lake, Michael Giles and Peter Sinfield. © Copyright 1969 and 1971 Enthoven Gaydon & Co., London, England. TRO-TOTAL MUSIC, INC., New York. Used by permission.

dirty to their elders, their indifference is often carefully calculated, their casualness studied in the mirror, and their dirty appearance based on a detailed imitation of their friends.

But the tyranny of fathers is not the same as the tyranny of one's peers. Not following fathers is quite different from not living up to the expectations of one's peers. The first means disobedience; the second, nonconformity. The first creates guilt feelings; the second, feelings of shame. In this respect there is an obvious shift from a guilt culture to a shame culture. This shift has very deep consequences, for if youth no longer aspires to become adult and take the place of the fathers, and if the main motivation is conformity to the peer group, we might witness the death of a future-oriented culture or—to use a theological term—the end of an eschatology. Then we no longer witness any desire to leave the safe place and to travel to the father's house which has so many rooms, any hope to reach the promised land or to see Him who is waiting for his prodigal son, any ambition to sit at the right or the left side of the heavenly throne. Then staying home, keeping in line and being in with your little group—becomes important. But that also is an absolute vote for the status quo.

This aspect of the coming generation raises serious questions for Christian leadership of tomorrow. But we would be getting a very one-sided picture as a basis for this leadership if we did not first take a careful look at the third aspect of the coming generation, called convulsiveness.

3. The convulsive generation

The inwardness and fatherlessness of the coming generation might lead us to expect a very quiet and contented future in which people keep to themselves and try to conform to their own little in-groups. But then we must take into account the fact that these attributes are closely related to a very deep-seated unhappiness with the society in which the young find themselves. Many young people are convinced that there is something terribly wrong with the world in which they live and that cooperation with existing models of living would constitute betrayal of themselves. Everywhere we see restless and nervous people, unable to concentrate and often suffering from a growing sense of depression. They know that what is shouldn't be the way it is, but they see no workable alternative. Thus they are saddled with frustration, which often expresses itself in undirected violence which destroys without clear purpose, or in suicidal withdrawal from the world, both of which are signs more of protest than of the results of a new-found ideal.

Immediately after the surrender of the exhausted state of Biafra, two high-school boys in France—Robert, nineteen years old, and Regis, sixteen years old—burned themselves to death and urged many of their peers to do the same. Interviews with their parents, pastors, teachers and friends revealed the horrifying fact that both of these sensitive students had become so overwhelmed by the hopeless misery of mankind and by the incapacity of adults to offer any real faith in a better world, that they chose to set their bodies afire as their ultimate way of protest.

To reach a better understanding of the underlying feelings of such students, let me quote from the letter of a student who had stopped studying and was still trying to find a new world. He wrote to his mother on January 1, 1970:

Society forces me to live an unfree life, to accept values which are not values to me. I reject the society as it now exists as a whole, but since I feel compassion for people living together, I try to look for alternatives. I have given myself the obligation to become aware of what it means to be a man and to search for the source of life. Church people call it "God." You see that I am traveling a difficult road to come to self-fulfillment, but I am proud that I seldom did what others expected me to do in line with a so-called "normal development." I really hope not to end up on the level of a square, chained to customs, traditions and the talk of next-door neighbors . . .

This letter seems to me a very sensitive expression of what many young people feel. They share a fundamental unhappiness with their world and a strong desire to work for change, but they doubt deeply that they will do better than their parents did, and almost completely lack any kind of vision or perspective. Within this framework I think that much erratic and undirected behavior is understandable. A man who feels caught like an animal in a trap may be dangerous and destructive, because of his undirected movements caused by his own panic.

This convulsive behavior is often misunderstood by those who have power and feel that society should be protected against protesting youth. They do not recognize the tremendous ambivalence behind much of this convulsive behavior, and rather than offering creative opportunities, they tend to polarize the situation and alienate even more those who are in fact only trying to find out what is worthwhile and what is not.

Similarly, sympathetic adults may misread the motives of the young. Riesman, in an article about radical students on campus, writes that many

> . . . *adults* fear to be thought old-fashioned or square and, by taking the part of the radical young without seeing the latter's own ambivalence, they are often no help to them but contribute to the severity of pressures from the peer group. And I expect to see that some faculty who have thought of themselves as very much on the side of students will themselves join the backlash when many students fail to reciprocate and are especially hostile towards the permissive faculty who have in the past been on their side. (*Psychology Today,* October 1969)

The generation to come is seeking desperately for a vision, an ideal to dedicate themselves to—a "faith," if you want. But their drastic language is often misunderstood and considered more a threat or a sturdy conviction than a plea for alternative ways of living.

Inwardness, fatherlessness and convulsiveness— these three characteristics of today's young people draw the first lines on the face of the coming generation. Now we are ready to ask what is expected of him who aspires to be a Christian leader in the world of tomorrow.

II. TOMORROW'S LEADER

When we look for the implications of our prognosis for the Christian ministry of the future, it appears as though three roles ask for special attention: (1) the leader as the articulator of inner events; (2) the leader

36

as man of compassion; (3) the leader as contemplative critic.

1. The minister as the articulator of inner events

The inward man is faced with a new and often dramatic task: He must come to terms with the inner tremendum. Since the God "out there" or "up there" is more or less dissolved in the many secular structures, the God within asks attention as never before. And just as the God outside could be experienced not only as a loving father but also as a horrible demon, the God within can be not only the source of a new creative life but also the cause of a chaotic confusion.

The greatest complaint of the Spanish mystics St. Teresa of Avila and St. John of the Cross was that they lacked a spiritual guide to lead them along the right paths and enable them to distinguish between creative and destructive spirits. We hardly need emphasize how dangerous the experimentation with the interior life can be. Drugs as well as different concentration practices and withdrawal into the self often do more harm than good. On the other hand it also is becoming obvious that those who avoid the painful encounter with the unseen are doomed to live a supercilious, boring and superficial life.

The first and most basic task required of the minister of tomorrow therefore is to clarify the immense confusion which can arise when people enter this new internal world. It is a painful fact indeed to realize how poorly prepared most Christian leaders prove to be when they are invited to be spiritual leaders in the true sense. Most of them are used to thinking in terms of large-scale organization, getting people together in churches, schools and hospitals, and running the show as a circus director. They have become unfamiliar with, and even somewhat afraid of, the deep and significant movements of the spirit. I am afraid that in a few decades the Church will be accused of having failed in its most basic task: to offer men creative ways to communicate with the source of human life.

But how can we avoid this danger? I think by no other way than to enter ourselves first of all into the center of our existence and become familiar with the complexities of our inner lives. As soon as we feel at home in our own house, discover the dark corners as well as the light spots, the closed doors as well as the drafty rooms, our confusion will evaporate, our anxiety will diminish, and we will become capable of creative work.

The key word here is articulation. The man who can articulate the movements of his inner life, who can give names to his varied experiences, need no longer be a victim of himself, but is able slowly and consistently to remove the obstacles that prevent the spirit from entering. He is able to create space for Him whose heart is greater than his, whose eyes see more than his, and whose hands can heal more than his.

This articulation, I believe, is the basis for a spiritual leadership of the future, because only he who is able to articulate his own experience can offer himself to others as a source of clarification. The Christian leader is, therefore, first of all, a man who is willing to put his own articulated faith at the disposal of those who ask his help. In this sense he is a servant of servants, because he is the first to enter the promised but dangerous land, the first to tell those who are afraid what he has seen, heard and touched.

This might sound highly theoretical, but the concrete consequences are obvious. In practically all priestly functions, such as pastoral conversation, preaching, teaching and liturgy, the minister tries to help people to recognize the work of God in themselves. The Christian leader, minister or priest, is not one who reveals God to his people—who gives something he has to those who have nothing—but one who helps those who are searching to discover reality as the source of their existence. In this sense we can say that the Christian leader leads man to confession, in the classic sense of the word: to the basic affirmation that man is man and God is God, and that without God, man cannot be called man.

In this context pastoral conversation is not merely a skillful use of conversational techniques to manipulate people into the Kingdom of God, but a deep human encounter in which a man is willing to put his own faith and doubt, his own hope and despair, his own light and darkness at the disposal of others who want to find a way through their confusion and touch the solid core of life. In this context preaching means more than handing over a tradition; it is rather the careful and sensitive articulation of what is happening in the community so that those who listen can say: "You say what I suspected, you express what I vaguely felt, you bring to the fore what I fearfully kept in the back of my mind. Yes, yes—you say who we are, you recognize our condition . . ."

When a listening man is able to say this, then the ground is broken for others to receive the Word of God. And no minister need doubt that the Word will be received! The young especially do not have to run away from their fears and hopes but can see themselves in the face of the man who leads them; he will make them understand the words of salvation which in the past often sounded to them like words from a strange and unfamiliar world.

Teaching in this context does not mean telling the old story over and over again, but the offering of channels through which people can discover themselves, clarify their own experiences and find the niches in which the Word of God can take firm hold. And finally, in this context liturgy is much more than ritual. It can become a true celebration when the liturgical leader is able to name the space where joy and sorrow touch each other as the place in which it is possible to celebrate both life and death.

So the first and most basic task of the Christian leader in the future will be to lead his people out of the land of confusion into the land of hope. Therefore, he must first have the courage to be an explorer of the new territory in himself and to articulate his discoveries as a service to the inward generation.

2. Compassion

By speaking about articulation as a form of leadership we have already suggested the place where the future leader will stand. Not "up there," far away or secretly hidden, but in the midst of his people, with the utmost visibility.

If we now realize that the future generation is not only an inward generation asking for articulation but also a fatherless generation looking for a new kind of authority, we must consider what the nature of this authority will be. To name it, I cannot find a better word than compassion. Compassion must become the core and even the nature of authority. When the Christian leader is a man of God for the future generation, he can be so only insofar as he is able to make the compassion of God with man—which is visible in Jesus Christ—credible in his own world.

The compassionate man stands in the midst of his people but does not get caught in the conformist forces of the peer group, because through his compassion he is able to avoid the distance of pity as well as the exclusiveness of sympathy. Compassion is born when we discover in the center of our own existence not only that God is God and man is man, but also that our neighbor is really our fellow man.

Through compassion it is possible to recognize that the craving for love that men feel resides also in our own hearts, that the cruelty that the world knows all too well is also rooted in our own impulses. Through compassion we also sense our hope for forgiveness in our friends' eyes and our hatred in their bitter mouths. When they kill, we know that we could have done it; when they give life, we know that we can do the same. For a compassionate man nothing human is alien: no joy and no sorrow, no way of living and no way of dying.

This compassion is authority because it does not tolerate the pressures of the in-group, but breaks through the boundaries between languages and countries, rich and poor, educated and illiterate. This compassion pulls people away from the fearful clique into the large world where they can see that every human face is the face of a neighbor. Thus the authority of compassion is the possibility of man to forgive his brother, because forgiveness is only real for him who has discovered the weakness of his friends and the sins of his enemy in his own heart and is willing to call every human being his brother. A fatherless generation looks for brothers who are able to take away their fear and anxiety, who can open the doors of their narrow-mindedness and show them that forgiveness is a possibility which dawns on the horizon of humanity.

The compassionate man who points to the possibility of forgiveness helps others to free themselves from the chains of their restrictive shame, allows them to experience their own guilt, and restores their hope for a future in which the lamb and the lion can sleep together.

But here we must be aware of the great temptation that will face the Christian minister of the future. Everywhere Christian leaders, men and women alike, have become increasingly aware of the need for more specific training and formation. This need is realistic, and the desire for more professionalism in the ministry is understandable. But the danger is that instead of becoming free to let the spirit grow, the future minister may entangle himself in the complications of his own assumed competence and use his specialism as an excuse to avoid the much more difficult task of being compassionate. The task of the Christian leader is to bring out the best in man and to lead him forward to a more human community; the danger is that his skillful diagnostic eye will become more an eye for distant and detailed analysis than the eye of a compassionate partner. And if priests and ministers of tomorrow think that more skill training is the solution for the problem of Christian leadership for the future generation, they may end up being more frustrated and disappointed than the leaders of today. More training and structure are just as necessary as more bread for the hungry. But just as bread given without love can bring war instead of peace, professionalism without compassion will turn forgiveness into a gimmick, and the kingdom to come into a blindfold.

This brings us to the final characteristic of the Christian leader of the future generation. If he is to be not just one in the long row of professionals who try to help man with their specific skills, if he is really to be an agent leading from confusion to hope and from chaos to harmony, he must be not only articulate and compassionate but a contemplative at heart as well.

3. The minister as contemplative man

We have said that the inward, fatherless generation desperately wants to change the world in which they live but tends to act spastically and convulsively in the face of a lack of a credible alternative. How can the Christian leader direct their explosive energy into creative channels and really be an agent of change? It might sound surprising and perhaps even contradictory, but I think that what is asked of the Christian leader of the future is that he be a contemplative critic.

I hope I will be able to prevent the free association of the word "contemplative" with a life lived behind walls, with a minimal contact with what is going on in the fast-moving world. What I have in mind is a very active, engaged form of contemplation of an evocative nature. This needs some explanation.

The man who does not know where he is going or what kind of world he is heading toward, who wonders if bringing forth children in this chaotic world is not an act of cruelty rather than love, will often be tempted to become sarcastic or even cynical. He laughs at his busy friends, but offers nothing in place of their activity. He protests against many things, but does not know what to witness for.

But the Christian minister who has discovered in himself the voice of the Spirit and has rediscovered his fellow men with compassion, might be able to look at the people he meets, the contacts he makes, and the events he becomes a part of, in a different way. He might reveal the first lines of the new world behind the veil of everyday life. As a contemplative critic he keeps a certain distance to prevent his becoming absorbed in what is most urgent and most immediate, but that same distance allows him to bring to the fore the real beauty of man and his world, which is always different, always fascinating, always new.

It is not the task of the Christian leader to go around nervously trying to redeem people, to save them at the last minute, to put them on the right track. For we are redeemed once and for all. The Christian leader is called to help others affirm this great news, and to make visible in daily events the fact that behind the dirty curtain of our painful symptoms there is something great to be seen: the face of Him in whose image we are shaped. In this way the contemplative can be a leader for a convulsive generation because he can break through the vicious circle of immediate needs asking for immediate satisfaction. He can direct the eyes of those who want to look beyond their impulses, and steer their erratic energy into creative channels.

Here we see that the future Christian minister can in no way be considered one concerned only about helping individuals to adapt themselves to a demanding world. In fact, the Christian leader who is able to be a critical contemplative will be a revolutionary in the most real sense. Because by testing all he sees, hears and touches for its evangelical authenticity, he is able to change the course of history and lead his people away from their panic-stricken convulsions to the creative action that will make a better world. He does not shoulder every protest sign in order to be in with those who express their frustration more than their ideas, nor does he easily join those asking for more protection, more police, more discipline and more order. But he will look critically at what is going on and make his decision based on insight into his own vocation, not on the desire for popularity or the fear of rejection. He will criticize the protesters as well as the rest seekers when their motives are false and their objectives dubious.

The contemplative is not needy or greedy for human contacts, but is guided by a vision of what he has seen beyond the trivial concerns of a possessive world. He does not bounce up and down with the fashions of the moment, because he is in contact with what is basic, central and ultimate. He does not allow anybody to worship idols, and he constantly invites his fellow man to ask real, often painful and upsetting questions, to look behind the surface of smooth behavior, and to take away all the obstacles that prevent him from getting to the heart of the matter. The contemplative critic takes away the illusory mask of the manipulative world and has the courage to show what the true situation is. He knows that he is considered by many as a fool, a madman, a danger to society and a threat to mankind. But he is not afraid to die, since his vision makes him transcend the difference between life and death and makes him free to do what has to be done here and now, notwithstanding the risks involved.

More than anything else, he will look for signs of hope and promise in the situation in which he finds himself. The contemplative critic has the sensibility to notice the small mustard seed and the trust to believe that "when it has grown it is the biggest shrub of all and becomes a tree so that the birds of the air come and shelter in its branches." (Mt. 13.31–32) He knows that if there is hope for a better world in the future the signs must be visible in the present, and he will

45

never curse the now in favor of the later. He is not a naïve optimist who expects his frustrated desires to be satisfied in the future, nor a bitter pessimist who keeps repeating that the past has taught him that there is nothing new under the sun; he is rather a man of hope who lives with the unshakable conviction that now he is seeing a dim reflection in a mirror, but that one day he will see the future face to face.

The Christian leader who is able not only to articulate the movements of the spirit but also to contemplate his world with a critical but compassionate eye, may expect that the convulsive generation will not choose death as the ultimate desperate form for protest, but instead the new life of which he has made visible the first hopeful signs.

CONCLUSION

We looked into the eyes of the young fugitive and found him inward, fatherless and convulsive. We wanted to prevent ourselves from handing him over to the enemy to be killed; we wanted instead to lead him to the center of our village and to recognize in this coming man the redeemer of a fearful world. To do this we are challenged to be articulate, compassionate and contemplative.

Is this too much of a task? Only if we feel we have to accomplish this individually and separately. But if anything has become clear in our day, it is that leadership is a shared vocation which develops by working closely together in a community where men and women can make each other realize that, as Teilhard de Chardin remarked, "to him who can see, nothing is profane."

Having said all this, I realize that I have done nothing more than rephrase the fact that the Christian leader must be in the future what he has always had to be in the past: a man of prayer, a man who has to pray, and who has to pray always. That I bring up this simple fact at this point may be surprising, but I hope I have succeeded in taking away all the sweet, pietistic, and churchy aura attached to this often misused word.

For a man of prayer is, in the final analysis, the man who is able to recognize in others the face of the Messiah and make visible what was hidden, make touchable what was unreachable. The man of prayer is a leader precisely because through his articulation of God's work within himself he can lead others out of confusion to clarification; through his compassion he can guide them out of the closed circuits of their in-groups to the wide world of humanity; and through his critical contemplation he can convert their convulsive destructiveness into creative work for the new world to come.

CHAPTER III

MINISTRY TO A HOPELESS MAN

Waiting for Tomorrow

INTRODUCTION

When we think about leadership we usually think about one man offering ideas, suggestions or directions to many others. We think of Mahatma Gandhi, Martin Luther King, John F. Kennedy, Dag Hammarskjold, Charles de Gaulle—all men who played an important role in modern history and found themselves at the center of public attention. But when we want to determine what kind of leadership a Christian can claim for himself, it sometimes seems better to start closer to home. There one has no chance to hide behind the excuse that one is not striving for worldwide change.

There is hardly a man or woman who does not exercise some leadership over other men or women. Among parents and children, teachers and students, bosses and employees, many different patterns of leadership can be found. In less formal settings—playgrounds, street gangs, academic and social societies, hobby and sports clubs—we also see how much of our life is dependent on the way leadership is given and accepted.

In this chapter I would like to concentrate on the simplest structure in which leadership plays a role: the encounter between two people. In this one-to-one relationship, we realize that we are involved in leading one another from point to point, from view to view, from one conviction to another. We need not name men like Hitler or Gandhi to demonstrate how destructive or creative this leadership can be. Even in the simple form of a conversation between two people, leadership can be a question of life and death. Indeed, in precisely this one-to-one encounter we discover some of the principles of Christian leadership, which also have implications for more complex leadership relationships.

Let a short conversation between a hospital patient and his visitor serve as a starting point for our discussion. The patient, Mr. Harrison, is a forty-eight-year-old farm laborer, stocky, tough-looking and not used to expressing himself verbally. He comes from a very simple Baptist family and feels completely disoriented in the big-city hospital where he was brought for an operation on his legs. He suffers from an insufficient functioning of his arteries. The visitor, John Allen, is a theology student who is taking a year of clinical-pastoral training under the supervision of the hospital chaplain.

This is John's second visit to Mr. Harrison. The patient sits in a wheelchair in the middle of the ward; other patients are present, some of them talking with each other. The following conversation takes place:

JOHN: Mr. Harrison, I'm . . . I came by . . . to see you the other day.

MR. HARRISON: O yes, I remember.

JOHN: How are things going?

MR. HARRISON: Well, I'll tell you. They were supposed to operate on me last week. They got me drugged, took me up there and my heart flew up. They de-

52

cided they'd better not try it then. They brought me back down here and I'm supposed to have the operation tomorrow.

JOHN: You say your heart flew up?

MR. HARRISON: Yes, they thought it might be too risky to go through with it. [PAUSE] I guess I'm ready for the operation. I think I can make it.

JOHN: You feel you're ready for it.

MR. HARRISON: Well, I'm not ready to die. But I think the operation is necessary or I'll lose my legs.

JOHN: You're not ready for the end, but you want something to be done if possible so you won't lose your legs.

MR. HARRISON: Yeah [nodding]. If this is the end, this is one who's gonna be lost.

JOHN: You feel the cause is lost if you don't make it through the operation.

MR. HARRISON: Yeah! Of course they tell me there's not too much to the operation. They're gonna dope me up right here and keep me here until it's time for the operation. They said they're going to put some plastic tubes inside me and that oughta save my legs. You see my foot here [takes shoe off and shows his foot]. This toe here gets blue when I stand on it. They could amputate here by the ankle, but this way they might save my legs.

JOHN: It's worth the operation if you can use your legs again.

MR. HARRISON: Yeah. Course I don't want to die during the operation. I'd rather die a natural death than die through anesthesia.

JOHN: You know the possibility of death is present during the operation, but the only way you can get well is to have the operation.

MR. HARRISON: Yeah, that's right.

Pause.

JOHN: You got much waiting for you when you leave the hospital?

MR. HARRISON: Nothing and nobody. Just hard work.

JOHN: Just a lot of hard labor.

MR. HARRISON: Yeah, that's right. Course I got to gain my strength back. I figure I'll be ready about the time the tobacco crop is ready.

JOHN: You'll be working with the tobacco crop?

MR. HARRISON: Yeah, picking starts around August.

JOHN: Mmm-hm.

Pause

JOHN: Well, Mr. Harrison, I hope things go well for you tomorrow.

MR. HARRISON: Thank you. Thanks for coming by.

JOHN: I'll be seeing you. Good-by.

MR. HARRISON: Good-by.

John did not speak to Mr. Harrison again. The next day, during the operation, Mr. Harrison died. Perhaps we might better say: "He never woke up from the anesthesia."

John had been asked to guide Mr. Harrison in this critical moment, to lead him to a new tomorrow. And what did "tomorrow" mean? For Mr. Harrison it meant a beginning of his return to the tobacco crop, or . . . an entry into the realm beyond death.

In order to come to a deeper understanding of the meaning of Christian leadership we will study in more detail the encounter between Mr. Harrison and John Allen. First we will consider Mr. Harrison's condition, then we will raise the question how John could have led Mr. Harrison to tomorrow. Finally we will discuss the main principles of Christian leadership which became visible in this encounter.

I. THE CONDITION OF MR. HARRISON

John was irritated and even a little angry when he came to the chaplain supervisor shortly after his visit to Mr. Harrison. He had the feeling that Mr. Harrison was a stubborn, indifferent man, with whom a decent conversation was hardly possible. He did not believe that Mr. Harrison had really appreciated his visit, and felt that in his bitter and somewhat coarse way of talking this patient had in fact expressed more hostility toward his visitor than gratitude. John was disappointed and did not hesitate to call Mr. Harrison an impossible man, that is, not a likely candidate for pastoral help.

John's reaction is quite understandable. As a young theology student he had hoped for a meaningful conversation with his patient, in which he could offer some hope and consolation. But he had felt frustrated, let down, and unable to "get anywhere." Only when he started to write, read and reread his conversation and to discuss with his supervisor what had actually happened, was he able to develop the distance necessary to see the painful condition of Mr. Harrison. Through that distance he could see that Mr. Harrison found himself in an impersonal-mechanical situation, afraid to die, but also afraid to live again. It is this paralyzing condition which John had to feel and taste deeply before he could be of help.

1. The impersonal milieu

For a theology student who went through grade school, high school, college and divinity school, it was

55

hard to imagine what it meant for a forty-eight-year-old man to be placed in the middle of the technocracy of a modern hospital. It must have been like coming to another planet where the people dress, behave, talk and act in a frightfully strange way. The white nurses, with their efficient way of washing, feeding and dressing patients; the doctors with their charts, making notes and giving orders in an utterly strange language; the many unidentifiable machines with bottles and tubes; and all the strange odors, noises, and foods must have made Mr. Harrison feel like a little child who has lost his way in a fearful forest. For him nothing was familiar, nothing understandable, nothing even approachable. Suddenly this tough man who could maintain his own independence through hard manual labor found himself the passive victim of many people and operations which were totally alien to him. He had lost control over himself. An anonymous group of "they people" had taken over: *"They* got me drugged, took me up there . . . *they* decided they better not try it then. *They* brought me back down here . . ."

This language shows that Mr. Harrison felt that strange powers had taken away his identity. The operation on his legs became a mysterious otherworldly manipulation. His own presence seemed unwanted in the process:

"They're gonna dope me up right here and keep me here until it's time for the operation. They said they're gonna put some plastic tubes inside me and that oughta save my legs."

For Mr. Harrison, "they" were working as if his very presence were only an incidental fact. No self-initiative was required or appreciated, no question expected or answered, no interest respected or stimulated. In Mr. Harrison's own experience: "They do things to it."

It was in this impersonal milieu that John Allen desired to offer his pastoral help.

2. The fear of death

While studying the verbatim report of his conversation with Mr. Harrison, John discovered that death had been at the center of his patient's concern. In some way Mr. Harrison had realized that his condition was a matter of life and death. Three times during their short interchange Mr. Harrison spoke about his fear of death, while John seemed constantly to avoid the subject or at least to cover up its painful reality.

Mr. Harrison feared an impersonal death, a death in which he did not have a part, of which he was not aware, and which was more real in the minds of the many powers around him than in his own mind.

Mr. Harrison must have sensed that the opportunity to die as a man was to be denied him: "Course I don't want to die during the operation. I'd rather die a natural death than die through anesthesia." Mr. Harrison realized that in the mechanical, incomprehensible milieu to which "they" brought him, his death was but a part of the process of human manipulaton to which he remained an outsider. There was a moment of protest in his hopeless remark. He, a man from the fields who had worked hard to make a living, who had had to rely wholly on his own body, knew that he had a right to die his own death, a natural death. He wanted to die the way he had lived. But his protest was weak and he must have realized that there was no choice. He would just vanish, slip away, stop living in a dreamlike state brought on by those who were going "to dope him up." He knew that if he died, he would be absent in that most crucial moment of human existence. It was not just the possibility of death during the operation which frightened Mr. Harrison, but also the fact that a chance to make death his own would be taken away from him, that in fact he would not die but simply fail to regain consciousness.

But there is more, much more. Mr. Harrison was not ready to die. Twice he tried to make his utter despair known to John, but John did not hear him. When John said, "You feel like you're ready for it," meaning the operation, Mr. Harrison revealed what was really on his mind: "Well, I'm not ready to die. . . . If this is the end, this is one who's gonna be lost." We can only guess what lay behind these desperate words full of agony and despair. Perhaps something too difficult for John to address. He tried to soften the hard realities. He called death "the end," and transformed "this is one who's gonna be lost" into "the cause." By softening the words of Mr. Harrison, John evaded confrontation with the personal agony of his patient.

Nobody can understand all the implications of Mr. Harrison's cry: "If this is the end, this is one who's gonna be lost." For what does "being lost" really mean? We do not know, but his Baptist background and his rough, lonely life imply that he might well have been speaking about being condemned, facing an eternal life in hell. This forty-eight-year-old man, without family or friends, without anybody around to talk with him, to understand or forgive him, faced death with the burden of a painful past on his shoulders. We have no idea of the many images which came to his mind at this hour, but a man as lonely and desperate as Mr. Harrison probably could not draw on past experiences that had established in him an awareness of God's love and forgiveness. Further, if the hour of death often brings back early memories, it might well be that the Baptist

58

sermons of his childhood, threatening with eternal punishment the man who yields to the "pleasures of this world," returned with horrifying vividness, forcing Mr. Harrison to identify himself in retrospect as "one who's gonna be lost." Maybe Mr. Harrison had not visited a church for years and had not met a minister since he was a boy. When the young chaplain, John, appeared at his wheelchair, it is likely that all the warnings, prohibitions, and admonitions of his childhood returned to him, and made the transgressions of his adulthood seem a heavy burden that could only lead to hell.

We do not know what really took place in Mr. Harrison's mind; however, there is no reason to underestimate the agonizing quality of his own words. Our "maybes" and "perhapses" can at least make us aware of what it means for a man to bring his forty-eight years of life to the day of judgment.

"I'm not ready to die." This means that Mr. Harrison was not prepared for a faithful act of surrender. He was not prepared to give his life away in faith and hope. His present suffering was small compared with what he expected beyond the boundary of life. Mr. Harrison feared death in the most existential way. But did he desire to live?

3. The fear of life

There are few patients who do not hope for a recovery when they face an operation. The complex hospital industry exists to heal, to restore, to bring people back to "normal life." Everyone who has paid a visit to a hospital and talked with patients knows that "tomorrow" means the day closer to home, to old friends, to the job, to everyday life. General hospitals are places that people want and expect to leave as soon as possible. It is in this context—the context of the healing power of human hope—that doctors, nurses, and aides do their work.

A man who does not want to leave the hospital does not cooperate with the over-all purpose of the institution and limits the power of all those who want to help him. Did Mr. Harrison strive to recuperate? We know he was afraid to die; however, that does not mean he wanted to live. Returning to normal life means in part returning to those who are waiting for you. But who was waiting for Mr. Harrison? John sensed Mr. Harrison's loneliness when he asked, "You got much waiting for you when you leave the hospital?" This question opened a deep wound, and Mr. Harrison replied, "Nothing and nobody. Just hard work."

It is very difficult if not impossible for a healthy young man to realize what it means when nobody cares whether you live or die. Isolation is among the worst of human sufferings, and for a man like John the experience of isolation is endless miles away. He has his supervisor to talk to, his friends to share his ideas with, his family and all the people who in one way or another are interested in his well-being. In contrast, what is life to one for whom no one waits, who expects only hard work in the tobacco crop, whose only motive for cure is to recover enough strength for the picking season? Certainly life does not call, does not pull the isolation away from the destructive processes in his body. Why should Mr. Harrison return to life?

Only to spend a few more years struggling in the hot sun to make just enough money to feed and dress himself until he is considered unfit for hard labor and can die a "natural death"? Death may be hell, but life no less.

Mr. Harrison did not really want to live any longer.

He feared that life which gave him so little happiness and so much pain. His legs hurt and he knew that without legs there was no life for him. But his legs couldn't bring him love; they promised only hard work, and that was a frightening thought.

Thus John found Mr. Harrison in an impersonal milieu, afraid to die and afraid to live. We do not know how serious Mr. Harrison's illness was, and we do not know how much chance he had to survive the operation. But Mr. Harrison was not ready for it. He did not understand what was going on around him; he wanted neither to die nor live. He was caught in a terrible trap. Any option would have been fatal, condemnation either to hell or to hard work.

This was Mr. Harrison's condition. Like many, he suffered from a psychic paralysis in which his deepest aspirations were cut, his desires blocked, his strivings frustrated, his will chained. Instead of a man filled with love and hate, desire and anger, hope and doubt, he had become a passive victim unable to give any direction to his own history. When the hands of doctors touch a man in this condition they touch a body which no longer speaks a language and has given up every form of cooperation. He cannot struggle to win the battle of life, or surrender peacefully, if his chances to win diminish. Under the surgeon's hands Mr. Harrison indeed did not have a name, nor did he claim one for himself. He had become an anonymous body which had even lost the ability to live. It simply stopped functioning.

As we all know, Mr. Harrison's is not an isolated case. Many people are the prisoners of their own existence. Mr. Harrison's condition is the condition of all men and women who do not understand the world in which they find themselves, and for whom death as well as life is loaded with fear.

And there are many like John as well. There are many idealistic, intelligent men and women who want to make others free and lead them to tomorrow. How then to free people like Mr. Harrison from their paralysis and lead them to tomorrow when a new life can start? This is the question we now have to consider.

II. HOW TO LEAD MR. HARRISON TO TOMORROW

John visited Mr. Harrison. The obvious question is: What could or should John have done for Mr. Harrison? But this question is really not fair. For the condition of Mr. Harrison was not immediately clear and comprehensible. Perhaps even now, after many hours of careful analysis of this short interchange, we still have nothing but a very partial understanding of what was happening to the patient. It is too easy to criticize the responses of John and to show how often he failed to come close to Mr. Harrison. What we in fact see is a serious attempt by John to listen to Mr. Harrison and to apply the rules of nondirective counseling which he learned in class. It is academic, awkward, and obviously filled with feelings of fear, hesitation, confusion, self-preoccupation, and distance. John and Mr. Harrison represent two worlds so different in history, thought, and feeling that it is totally unrealistic, if not inhuman, to expect that they would be able to understand each other in two rather casual conversations. It is even pretentious to think that we, with our academic distinctions, will ever know who this farm worker was and how he faced his death. The mystery of one man is too immense and too profound to be explained by another man. And still the question: "How could Mr. Harrison be led to tomorrow?" is a valid question. For one man needs another to live, and the deeper he is willing to enter into the painful condition which he and others know, the more likely it is that he can be a leader, leading his people out of the desert into the promised land.

Therefore, what follows is not a lesson to show John how miserably he failed to help Mr. Harrison and to tell him what he should have done, but an attempt to recognize in Mr. Harrison's condition the agony of all men: man's desperate cry for a human response from his brother.

Probably John couldn't have done much more than he did during his talk with Mr. Harrison, but the study of this tragic human situation may reveal that indeed man's response is a matter of life and death.

The response which might have been within the reach of human possibility is a personal response in an impersonal milieu, by which one man can wait for another in life as well as in death.

1. A personal response

When theology students read the conversation between John and Mr. Harrison, they usually have strong criticism toward John's responses and offer ideas about what they themselves might have said. They explain: "I would have told him to think about the good experiences he had in life and would have attempted to offer him hope for a better life," or: "I would have explained to him that God is merciful and will forgive him his sins," or: "I would have tried to find out more about the nature of his illness and showed him that he really had a good chance to recover," or: "I would have talked more with him about his fear to die and would have talked about his past so that he could unburden his guilty conscience," or: "I would have talked about death as a way to new life for a man who can put his faith in Christ."

All these and other proposed responses are grounded in a deep desire to help and to offer a message of hope which can alleviate the pains of this suffering man. But still the question remains: "What use can an illiterate man in the hour of agony make of the words, explanations, exhortations and arguments of a theology student? Can anyone change a man's ideas, feelings or perspectives a few hours before his death? To be sure, forty-eight years of living are not ruffled by a few intelligent remarks by a well-meaning seminarian. John may have been too nondirective, he may have lacked the courage for clear witness or for deeper concern. But what difference would it really have made?

The possibilities of John's visit to Mr. Harrison will never be made manifest if we expect any salvation from a change in terminology, or a new twist in the order or the nature of the words we use. We might even ask ourselves: "Wouldn't it have been better for John to stay away from Mr. Harrison, to leave him alone, to prevent him from making morbid associations with the appearance of a preacher?"

Yes . . . unless in the middle of the anonymity caused by his surroundings Mr. Harrison were to meet a man with a clear face who called him by his name and became his brother . . . unless John were to become a person Mr. Harrison could see, touch, smell, and hear, and whose real presence would in no way be denied. If a man were to appear from out of the cloudiness of Mr. Harrison's existence who looked at him, spoke to him, and pressed his hands in a gesture of real concern, that would have mattered. The emptiness of the past and the future can never be filled with words but only by the presence of a man. Because only then can the hope be born, that there might be at least one exception to the "nobody and nothing" of his complaint—a hope that will make him whisper, "Maybe, after all, someone is waiting for me."

2. *Waiting in life*

Nobody can offer leadership to anyone unless he makes his presence known—that is, unless he steps forward out of the anonymity and apathy of his milieu and makes the possibility of fellowship visible.

But how could John, even when really present to Mr. Harrison, even when able to express his real concern to him, lead him out of his fear into the hope for tomorrow? We might as well start by realizing that neither John nor any other concerned person would want Mr. Harrison to die. The operation was meant to save his legs, and when Mr. Harrison said, "I think I can make it," only a heartless man would have criticized his careful guess. For a patient facing surgery, tomorrow must be the day of recovery, not the day of death.

John's task was therefore to strengthen his patient's desire to recover and to reinforce what little strength he had in the struggle for life.

But how? By making Mr. Harrison's dangerous generalization, "Nothing and nobody is waiting for me," untrue, by reducing it to a paralyzing self-complaint; and by a frontal attack against his false self-concept: "Look at me, and try to say that again—you will see in my eyes that you are wrong—I am here, and I am waiting for you—I will be here tomorrow and the day after tomorrow—and you are not going to let me down."

No man can stay alive when nobody is waiting for him. Everyone who returns from a long and difficult trip is looking for someone waiting for him at the station or the airport. Everyone wants to tell his story and share his moments of pain and exhilaration with someone who stayed home, waiting for him to come back.

Alexander Berkman, the anarchist who attempted to kill the industrial captain Henry Clay Frick in 1892, would have gone insane during his fourteen years of brutal prison life had there not been a few friends waiting for him outside. (See *Prison Memoirs of an Anarchist* by Alexander Berkman, New York, 1970.) George Jackson, Soledad brother, who was imprisoned in 1960 when he was eighteen years old for robbing a gas station of $70, and who was killed in 1971 while trying to escape, would never have been able to write the impressive human document he did write if his mother, his father, his brothers Robert and Jonathan, and his friend Fay Stender had not been waiting outside, receiving his letters and constantly reacting to his thoughts. (See *Soledad Brother, The Prison Letters of George Jackson,* New York, 1970.)

A man can keep his sanity and stay alive as long as there is at least one person who is waiting for him. The mind of man can indeed rule his body even when there is little health left. A dying mother can stay alive to see her son before she gives up the stuggle, a soldier can prevent his mental and physical disintegration when he knows that his wife and children are waiting for him. But when "nothing and nobody" is waiting, there is no chance to survive in the struggle for life. Mr. Harrison had no reason to come out of the anesthesia if returning to consciousness meant arriving at a station where thousands of people ran left and right, but where no one raised his hand, approached him with a smile of recognition or welcomed him back into the land of the living. John might have been that one man. He might have saved Mr. Harrison's life by making him realize that returning to life is a gift to him who is waiting. Thousands of people commit suicide because there is nobody waiting for them tomorrow. There is no reason to live if there is nobody to live for.

But when a man says to his fellow man, "I will not let you go. I am going to be here tomorrow waiting for you and I expect you not to disappoint me," then tomorrow is no longer an endless dark tunnel. It becomes flesh and blood in the brother who is waiting and for whom he wants to give life one more chance. When tomorrow only meant the tobacco crop and hard labor and a lonely life, Mr. Harrison could hardly have been expected to cooperate with the surgeon's work. But if John had stood on the threshold of tomorrow, Mr. Harrison might have wanted to know what he would have to say about the day after, and have given the doctor a helping hand.

Let us not diminish the power of waiting by saying that a lifesaving relationship cannot develop in an hour. One eye movement or one handshake can replace years of friendship when man is in agony. Love not only lasts forever, it needs only a second to come about.

John might indeed have saved Mr. Harrison's life by becoming his tomorrow.

3. Waiting in death

But Mr. Harrison's recovery was far from sure. Mr. Harrison himself was the first to realize this. Three times he explicitly spoke about his death, and he knew that his illness was serious enough to question a positive outcome from the operation. In the short interchange with John Allen, Mr. Harrison seemed to fear death even more than a return to life. Does not John's presence and faithful waiting become ridiculous in the face of a man who quite possibly will not live the next day? Many patients have been fooled with stories about recovery and the better life after that, while few consoling people believed in their own words. What sense does it make to speak about waiting for tomorrow when those words will quite likely be the last words spoken to the patient?

Here we touch upon the most sensitive spot of John's encounter with Mr. Harrison. Why should a healthy-looking, intelligent man show himself and make himself really present to a man in whom the forces of death are at work? What does it mean for a dying man to be confronted with another man for whom life has hardly begun? This looks like psychological torture, in which a dying man is reminded by a young fellow that his life could have been so different, but that it is too late to change.

Most people in our society do not want to disturb each other with the idea of death. They want a man to die without ever having realized that death was approaching. Surely John could not lead Mr. Harrison to tomorrow by playing this false game. Instead of leading him he would have been misleading him. He would have stolen his human right to die.

In truth, can John really say, "I will be waiting for you," if this would only be true in the case of Mr. Harrison's recovery? Or can one man wait for another man, whatever happens to him, death included? In the face of death there is hardly any difference between John and Mr. Harrison. They will both die. The difference is time, but what does time mean when two people have discovered each other as fellow men? If John's waiting could have saved Mr. Harrison's life, the power of his waiting would not be conditioned by Mr. Harrison's recovery, because when two people have become present to each other, the waiting of one must be able to cross the narrow line between the living or dying of the other.

Mr. Harrison was afraid to die, because he was afraid of condemnation, of an eternal prolongation of his isolation. Whatever else hell may mean to Mr. Harrison, it certainly entails his total rejection. But were he able to accept John's presence, he might have felt that someone at least protested against his fear and that in the hour of death he was not alone.

It is indeed possible for man to be faithful in death, to express a solidarity based not just on a return to everyday life, but also on a participation in the death experience which belongs in the center of the human heart. "I will be waiting for you" means much more than, "If you make it through the operation I will be there to be with you again." There will be no "ifs." "I will wait for you" goes beyond death and is the deepest expression of the fact that faith and hope may pass but that love will remain forever. "I will wait for you" is an expression of solidarity which breaks through the chains of death. At that moment John is no longer a chaplain trying to do a good piece of counseling, and Mr. Harrison is no longer a farm worker doubting if he will make it through the operation; rather they are two men who reawaken in each other the deepest human intuition, that life is eternal and cannot be made futile by a biological process.

One can lead another to tomorrow even when tomorrow is the day of the other's death, because he can wait for him on both sides. But would it have been so meaningful for John to have led Mr. Harrison back to the tobacco crop if this was just another delay for a man on death row?

Man protests against death, for he is not content with a postponement of the execution. And it is this protest that might have mobilized in Mr. Harrison both the powers of recovery and the ability to break through the wall of his fears, making his death an entry into a life where he is awaited. So perhaps John might indeed have led Mr. Harrison to tomorrow by making himself present to him and waiting for him in life and death. Indeed, it is exactly the willingness of John to enter with Mr. Harrison into his paralyzing condition which would have enabled him to be a guide or leader in the best sense. Only by this personal participation could he have freed Mr. Harrison of his paralysis and made him responsible again for his own history. In this sense he indeed could save Mr. Harrison's life, whether or not that entails recovery. With John waiting, the surgeon would not have had to work on a passive victim, but with a man able to make decisions that count.

Mr. Harrison's condition is more than the condition of one man in a particular hospital. It is indeed an image of the condition of all. The leadership potential is not just a possibility to be actualized by a well-trained theologian, but the responsibility of every Christian. Therefore let us now finally discuss the main principles of Christian leadership which become visible in this encounter.

III. PRINCIPLES OF CHRISTIAN LEADERSHIP

How could we speak about Christian leadership without mentioning Jesus Christ, His life, His

70

crucifixion and His resurrection? The only answer is: He has been here from the first page of this chapter. The understanding of Mr. Harrison's condition and the search for a creative response were based on God's revelation in Jesus Christ. This revelation shows in the paralyzing condition of Mr. Harrison, the condition of man. It also reveals to us the possibility of following Christ in a faithful waiting for another beyond the boundaries which separate life from death. Therefore we can discover and rediscover in the encounter between Mr. Harrison and John the basic principles of Christian leadership: first, personal concern, which asks one man to give his life for his fellow man; second, a deep-rooted faith in the value and meaning of life, even when the days look dark; and third, an outgoing hope which always looks for tomorrow, even beyond the moment of death. And all these principles are based on the one and only conviction that, since God has become man, it is man who has the power to lead his fellow man to freedom. Let us now pay special attention to these three principles which we derived from John's visit to Mr. Harrison.

1. Personal concern

If there is any posture that disturbs a suffering man or woman, it is aloofness. The tragedy of Christian ministry is that many who are in great need, many who seek an attentive ear, a word of support, a forgiving embrace, a firm hand, a tender smile, or even a stuttering confession of inability to do more, often find their ministers distant men who do not want to burn their fingers. They are unable or unwilling to express their feelings of affection, anger, hostility or sympathy. The paradox indeed is that those who want to be for "everyone" find themselves often unable to be close to anyone. When everybody becomes my "neighbor," it is worth wondering whether anybody can really become my "proximus," that is, the one who is most close to me.

After so much stress on the necessity of a leader to prevent his own personal feelings and attitudes from interfering in a helping relationship (see the excellent study by Seward Hiltner: *Counselor on Counseling*. Nashville, Tennessee, Abingdon, 1950) it seems necessary to re-establish the basic principle that no one can help anyone without becoming involved, without entering with his whole person into the painful situation, without taking the risk of becoming hurt, wounded or even destroyed in the process. The beginning and the end of all Christian leadership is to give your life for others. Thinking about martyrdom can be an escape unless we realize that real martyrdom means a witness that starts with the willingness to cry with those who cry, laugh with those who laugh, and to make one's own painful and joyful experiences available as sources of clarification and understanding.

Who can save a child from a burning house without taking the risk of being hurt by the flames? Who can listen to a story of loneliness and despair without taking the risk of experiencing similar pains in his own heart and even losing his precious peace of mind? In short: "Who can take away suffering without entering it?"

The great illusion of leadership is to think that man can be led out of the desert by someone who has never been there. Our lives are filled with examples which tell us that leadership asks for understanding and that understanding requires sharing. So long as we define leadership in terms of preventing or establishing precedents, or in terms of being responsible for some kind of abstract "general good," we have forgotten that no

God can save us except a suffering God, and that no man can lead his people except the man who is crushed by its sins. Personal concern means making Mr. Harrison the only one who counts, the one for whom I am willing to forget my many other obligations, my scheduled appointments and long-prepared meetings, not because they are not important but because they lose their urgency in the face of Mr. Harrison's agony. Personal concern makes it possible to experience that going after the "lost sheep" is really a service to those who were left alone.

Many will put their trust in him who went all the way, out of concern for just one of them. The remark "He really cares for us" is often illustrated by stories which show that forgetting the many for the one is a sign of true leadership.

It is not just curiosity which makes people listen to a preacher when he speaks directly to a man and a woman whose marriage he blesses or to the children of the man whom he buries in the ground. They listen in the deepseated hope that a personal concern might give the preacher words that carry beyond the ears of those whose joy or suffering he shares. Few listen to a sermon which is intended to be applicable to everyone, but most pay careful attention to words born out of concern for only a few.

All this suggests that when one has the courage to enter where life is experienced as most unique and most private, one touches the soul of the community. The man who has spent many hours trying to understand, feel, and clarify the alienation and confusion of one of his fellow men might well be the best equipped to speak to the needs of the many, because all men are one at the wellspring of pain and joy.

This is what Carl Rogers pointed out when he

73

wrote: ". . . I have—found that the very feeling which has seemed to me most private, most personal and hence most incomprehensible by others, has turned out to be an expression for which there is a resonance in many other people. It has led me to believe that what is most personal and unique in each one of us is probably the very element which would, if it were shared or expressed, speak most deeply to others. This has helped me to understand artists and poets who have dared to express the unique in themselves" (*On Becoming a Person*. London, 1961, p. 26). It indeed seems that the Christian leader is first of all the artist who can bind together many people by his courage in giving expression to his most personal concern.

2. *Faith in the value and meaning of life*

Faith in the value and meaning of life, even in the face of despair and death, is the second principle of Christian leadership. This seems so obvious that it is often taken for granted and overlooked.

John's visit to Mr. Harrison asks for a personal concern, but this concern can only be sustained by a growing faith in the value and meaning of the life which takes shape in the encounter itself. Christian leadership is a dead-end street when nothing new is expected, when everything sounds familiar and when ministry has regressed to the level of routine. Many have walked into that dead-end street and found themselves imprisoned in a life where all the words were already spoken, all events had already taken place, and all the people had already been met.

But for a man with a deep-rooted faith in the value and meaning of life, every experience holds a new promise, every encounter carries a new insight, and every event brings a new message. But these promises,

74

insights, and messages have to be discovered and made visible. A Christian leader is not a leader because he announces a new idea and tries to convince others of its worth; he is a leader because he faces the world with eyes full of expectation, with the expertise to take away the veil that covers its hidden potential. Christian leadership is called ministry precisely to express that in the service of others new life can be brought about. It is this service which gives eyes to see the flower breaking through the cracks in the street, ears to hear a word of forgiveness muted by hatred and hostility, and hands to feel new life under the cover of death and destruction. Mr. Harrison was not just a bitter and hostile man, resistant to pastoral help. For a real minister he incarnates the truth that it belongs to the dignity of man to die a human death, to surrender life instead of allowing it to be taken away from him in a state of unconsciousness. Underneath his coarse and bitter remarks, a Christian hears a cry for help in facing what is hidden behind his imminent death, and above all the cry for someone who will be with him in life and in death.

The encounter between these two men in a crisis situation therefore is not an accidental event but a direct appeal to both of them to discover or rediscover the basic search of the human heart. But this appeal can only be heard by one who has a deep-rooted faith in the value and meaning of life, by one who knows that life is not a static given but a mystery which reveals itself in the ongoing encounter between man and his world.

3. Hope

While personal concern is sustained by a continuously growing faith in the value and meaning of life, the deepest motivation for leading our fellow man to the future is hope. For hope makes it possible to look beyond the fulfillment of urgent wishes and pressing desires and offers a vision beyond human suffering and even death. A Christian leader is a man of hope whose strength in the final analysis is based neither on self-confidence derived from his personality, nor on specific expectations for the future, but on a promise given to him.

This promise not only made Abraham travel to unknown territory; it not only inspired Moses to lead his people out of slavery; it is also the guiding motive for any Christian who keeps pointing to new life even in the face of corruption and death.

Without this hope, we will never be able to see value and meaning in the encounter with a decaying human being and become personally concerned. This hope stretches far beyond the limitations of one's own psychological strength, for it is anchored not just in the soul of the individual but in God's self-disclosure in history. Leadership therefore is not called Christian because it is permeated with optimism against all the odds of life, but because it is grounded in the historic Christ-event which is understood as a definitive breach in the deterministic chain of human trial and error, and as a dramatic affirmation that there is light on the other side of darkness.

Every attempt to attach this hope to visible symptoms in our surroundings becomes a temptation when it prevents us from the realization that promises, not concrete successes, are the basis of Christian leadership. Many ministers, priests and Christian laymen have become disillusioned, bitter and even hostile when years of hard work bear no fruit, when little change is accomplished. Building a vocation on the expectations of concrete results, however conceived, is like building a house on sand instead of on solid rock, and even takes away the ability to accept successes as free gifts.

Hope prevents us from clinging to what we have and frees us to move away from the safe place and enter unknown and fearful territory. This might sound romantic, but when a man enters with his fellow man into his fear of death and is able to wait for him right there, "leaving the safe place" might turn out to be a very difficult act of leadership. It is an act of discipleship in which we follow the hard road of Christ, who entered death with nothing but bare hope.

CONCLUSION

Thus, waiting for tomorrow, as an act of Christian leadership, asks for personal concern, a deep faith in the value and meaning of life, and a strong hope which breaks through the boundaries of death. In this analysis it has become clear that Christian leadership is accomplished only through service. This service requires the willingness to enter into a situation, with all the human vulnerabilities a man has to share with his fellow man. This is a painful and self-denying experience, but an experience which can indeed lead man out of his prison of confusion and fear. Indeed, the paradox of Christian leadership is that the way out is the way in, that only by entering into communion with human suffering can relief be found. As John was invited to enter into Mr. Harrison's agony and wait for him there, every Christian is constantly invited to overcome his neighbor's fear by entering into it with him, and to find in the fellowship of suffering the way to freedom.

77

CHAPTER IV

MINISTRY BY A LONELY MINISTER

The Wounded Healer

INTRODUCTION

In the middle of our convulsive world men and women raise their voices time and again to announce with incredible boldness that we are waiting for a Liberator. We are waiting, they announce, for a Messiah who will free us from hatred and oppression, from racism and war—a Messiah who will let peace and justice take their rightful place.

If the ministry is meant to hold the promise of this Messiah, then whatever we can learn of His coming will give us a deeper understanding of what is called for in ministry today.

How does our Liberator come? I found an old legend in the Talmud which may suggest to us the beginning of an answer:

> Rabbi Yoshua ben Levi came upon Elijah the prophet while he was standing at the entrance of Rabbi Simeron ben Yohai's cave . . . He asked Elijah, "When will the Messiah come?" Elijah replied,
> "Go and ask him yourself."
> "Where is he?"

"Sitting at the gates of the city."

"How shall I know him?"

"He is sitting among the poor covered with wounds. The others unbind all their wounds at the same time and then bind them up again. But he unbinds one at a time and binds it up again, saying to himself, 'Perhaps I shall be needed: if so I must always be ready so as not to delay for a moment.'" (Taken from the tractate Sanhedrin)

The Messiah, the story tells us, is sitting among the poor, binding his wounds one at a time, waiting for the moment when he will be needed. So it is too with the minister. Since it is his task to make visible the first vestiges of liberation for others, he must bind his own wounds carefully in anticipation of the moment when he will be needed. He is called to be the wounded healer, the one who must look after his own wounds but at the same time be prepared to heal the wounds of others.

He is both the wounded minister and the healing minister, two concepts I would like to explore in this last chapter.

I. THE WOUNDED MINISTER

The Talmud story suggests that, because he binds his own wounds one at a time, the Messiah would not have to take time to prepare himself if asked to help someone else. He would be ready to help. Jesus has given this story a new fullness by making his own broken body the way to health, to liberation and new life. Thus like Jesus, he who proclaims liberation is called not only to care for his own wounds and the wounds of others, but also to make his wounds into a major source of his healing power.

But what are our wounds? They have been spoken about in many ways by many voices. Words such as "alienation," "separation," "isolation" and "loneliness" have been used as the names of our wounded condition. Maybe the word "loneliness" best expresses our immediate experience and therefore most fittingly enables us to understand our brokenness. The loneliness of the minister is especially painful; for over and above his experience as a man in modern society, he feels an added loneliness, resulting from the changing meaning of the ministerial profession itself.

1. Personal loneliness

We live in a society in which loneliness has become one of the most painful human wounds. The growing competition and rivalry which pervade our lives from birth have created in us an acute awareness of our isolation. This awareness has in turn left many with a heightened anxiety and an intense search for the experience of unity and community. It has also led people to ask anew how love, friendship, brotherhood and sisterhood can free them from isolation and offer them a sense of intimacy and belonging. All around us we see the many ways by which the people of the western world are trying to escape this loneliness. Psychotherapy, the many institutes which offer group experiences with verbal and nonverbal communication techniques, summer courses and conferences supported by scholars, trainers and "huggers" where people can share common problems, and the many experiments which seek to create intimate liturgies where peace is not only announced but also felt—these increasingly popular phenomena are all signs of a painful attempt to break through the immobilizing wall of loneliness.

But the more I think about loneliness, the more I think that the wound of loneliness is like the Grand Canyon—a deep incision in the surface of our existence which has become an inexhaustible source of beauty and self-understanding.

Therefore I would like to voice loudly and clearly what might seem unpopular and maybe even disturbing: The Christian way of life does not take away our loneliness; it protects and cherishes it as a precious gift. Sometimes it seems as if we do everything possible to avoid the painful confrontation with our basic human loneliness, and allow ourselves to be trapped by false gods promising immediate satisfaction and quick relief. But perhaps the painful awareness of loneliness is an invitation to transcend our limitations and look beyond the boundaries of our existence. The awareness of loneliness might be a gift we must protect and guard, because our loneliness reveals to us an inner emptiness that can be destructive when misunderstood, but filled with promise for him who can tolerate its sweet pain.

When we are impatient, when we want to give up our loneliness and try to overcome the separation and incompleteness we feel, too soon, we easily relate to our human world with devastating expectations. We ignore what we already know with a deep-seated, intuitive knowledge—that no love or friendship, no intimate embrace or tender kiss, no community, commune or collective, no man or woman, will ever be able to satisfy our desire to be released from our lonely condition. This truth is so disconcerting and painful that we are more prone to play games with our fantasies than to face the truth of our existence. Thus we keep hoping that one day we will find the man who really understands our experiences, the woman who will bring peace to our restless life, the job where we can fulfill our potentials, the book which will explain everything, and the place where we can feel at home. Such false hope leads us to make exhausting demands and prepares us for bitterness and dangerous hostility when we start discovering that nobody, and nothing, can live up to our absolutistic expectations.

Many marriages are ruined because neither partner was able to fulfill the often hidden hope that the other would take his or her loneliness away. And many celibates live with the naïve dream that in the intimacy of marriage their loneliness will be taken away.

When the minister lives with these false expectations and illusions he prevents himself from claiming his own loneliness as a source of human understanding, and is unable to offer any real service to the many who do not understand their own suffering.

2. Professional loneliness

The wound of loneliness in the life of the minister hurts all the more, since he not only shares in the human condition of isolation, but also finds that his professional impact on others is diminishing. The minister is called to speak to the ultimate concerns of life: birth and death, union and separation, love and hate. He has an urgent desire to give meaning to people's lives. But he finds himself standing on the edges of events and only reluctantly admitted to the spot where the decisions are made.

In hospitals, where many utter their first cry as well as their last words, ministers are often more tolerated than required. In prisons, where men's desire for liberation and freedom is most painfully felt, a chaplain feels like a guilty bystander whose words hardly move the wardens. In the cities, where children play between buildings and old people die isolated and forgotten, the protests of priests are hardly taken seriously and their demands hang in the air like rhetorical questions. Many churches decorated with words announcing salvation and new life are often little more than parlors for those who feel quite comfortable in the old life, and who are not likely to let the minister's words change their stone hearts into furnaces where swords can be cast into plowshares, and spears into pruning hooks.

The painful irony is that the minister, who wants to touch the center of men's lives, finds himself on the periphery, often pleading in vain for admission. He never seems to be where the action is, where the plans are made and the strategies discussed. He always seems to arrive at the wrong places at the wrong times with the wrong people, outside the walls of the city when the feast is over, with a few crying women.

A few years ago, when I was chaplain of the Holland-America line, I was standing on the bridge of a huge Dutch ocean liner which was trying to find its way through a thick fog into the port of Rotterdam. The fog was so thick, in fact, that the steersman could not even see the bow of the ship. The captain, carefully listening to a radar station operator who was explaining his position between other ships, walked nervously up and down the bridge and shouted his orders to the steersman. When he suddenly stumbled over me, he blurted out: "God damn it, Father, get out of my way." But when I was ready to run away, filled with feelings of incompetence and guilt, he came back and said: "Why don't you just stay around. This might be the only time I really need you."

There was a time, not too long ago, when we felt like

captains running our own ships with a great sense of power and self-confidence. Now we are standing in the way. That is our lonely position: We are powerless, on the side, liked maybe by a few crew members who swab the decks and goof off to drink a beer with us, but not taken very seriously when the weather is fine.

The wound of our loneliness is indeed deep. Maybe we had forgotten it, since there were so many distractions. But our failure to change the world with our good intentions and sincere actions and our undesired displacement to the edges of life have made us aware that the wound is still there.

So we see how loneliness is the minister's wound not only because he shares in the human condition, but also because of the unique predicament of his profession. It is this wound which he is called to bind with more care and attention than others usually do. For a deep understanding of his own pain makes it possible for him to convert his weakness into strength and to offer his own experience as a source of healing to those who are often lost in the darkness of their own misunderstood sufferings. This is a very hard call, because for a minister who is committed to forming a community of faith, loneliness is a very painful wound which is easily subject to denial and neglect. But once the pain is accepted and understood, a denial is no longer necessary, and ministry can become a healing service.

II. THE HEALING MINISTER

How can wounds become a source of healing? This is a question which requires careful consideration. For when we want to put our wounded selves in the service of others, we must consider the relationship between our professional and personal lives.

On the one hand, no minister can keep his own experience of life hidden from those he wants to help. Nor should he want to keep it hidden. While a doctor can still be a good doctor even when his private life is severely disrupted, no minister can offer service without a constant and vital acknowledgment of his own experiences. On the other hand, it would be very easy to misuse the concept of the wounded healer by defending a form of spiritual exhibitionism. A minister who talks in the pulpit about his own personal problems is of no help to his congregation, for no suffering human being is helped by someone who tells him that he has the same problems. Remarks such as, "Don't worry because I suffer from the same depression, confusion and anxiety as you do," help no one. This spiritual exhibitionism adds little faith to little faith and creates narrow-mindedness instead of new perspectives. Open wounds stink and do not heal.

Making one's own wounds a source of healing, therefore, does not call for a sharing of superficial personal pains but for a constant willingness to see one's own pain and suffering as rising from the depth of the human condition which all men share.

To some, the concept of the wounded healer might sound morbid and unhealthy. They might feel that the ideal of self-fulfillment is replaced by an ideal of self-castigation, and that pain is romanticized instead of criticized. I would like to show how the idea of the wounded healer does not contradict the concept of self-realization, or self-fulfillment, but deepens and broadens it.

How does healing take place? Many words, such as care and compassion, understanding and forgiveness, fellowship and community, have been used for the healing task of the Christian minister. I like to use the word hospitality, not only because it has such deep roots in the Judaeo-Christian tradition, but also, and primarily, because it gives us more insight into the nature of response to the human condition of loneliness. Hospitality is the virtue which allows us to break through the narrowness of our own fears and to open our houses to the stranger, with the intuition that salvation comes to us in the form of a tired traveler. Hospitality makes anxious disciples into powerful witnesses, makes suspicious owners into generous givers, and makes closed-minded sectarians into interested recipients of new ideas and insights.

But it has become very difficult for us today to fully understand the implications of hospitality. Like the Semitic nomads, we live in a desert with many lonely travelers who are looking for a moment of peace, for a fresh drink and for a sign of encouragement so that they can continue their mysterious search for freedom.

What does hospitality as a healing power require? It requires first of all that the host feel at home in his own house, and secondly that he create a free and fearless place for the unexpected visitor. Therefore, hospitality embraces two concepts: concentration and community.

1. Hospitality and concentration

Hospitality is the ability to pay attention to the guest. This is very difficult, since we are preoccupied with our own needs, worries and tensions, which prevent us from taking distance from ourselves in order to pay attention to others.

Not long ago I met a parish priest. After describing his hectic daily schedule—religious services, classroom teaching, luncheon and dinner engagements, and organizational meetings—he said apologetically: "Yes . . . but there are so many problems. . . ." When I asked, "Whose problems?" he was silent for a few minutes, and then more or less reluctantly said, "I guess—my own." Indeed, his incredible activities seemed in large part motivated by fear of what he would discover when he came to a standstill. He actually said: "I guess I am busy in order to avoid a painful self-concentration."

So we find it extremely hard to pay attention because of our intentions. As soon as our intentions take over, the question no longer is, "Who is he?" but, "What can I get from him?"—and then we no longer listen to what he is saying but to what we can do with what he is saying. Then the fulfillment of our unrecognized need for sympathy, friendship, popularity, success, understanding, money or a career becomes our concern, and instead of paying attention to the other person we impose ourselves upon him with intrusive curiosity. (See James Hillman: *Insearch*, Charles Scribner's Sons, New York, 1967, p. 18.)

Anyone who wants to pay attention without intention has to be at home in his own house—that is, he has to discover the center of his life in his own heart. Concentration, which leads to meditation and contemplation, is therefore the necessary precondition for true hospitality. When our souls are restless, when we are driven by thousands of different and often conflicting stimuli, when we are always "over there" between people, ideas and the worries of this world, how can we possibly create the room and space where someone else can enter freely without feeling himself an unlawful intruder?

90

Paradoxically, by withdrawing into ourselves, not out of self-pity but out of humility, we create the space for another to be himself and to come to us on his own terms. James Hillman, director of studies at the C. G. Jung Institute in Zurich, speaking about counseling, writes:

> For the other person to open and talk requires a withdrawal of the counselor. I must withdraw to make room for the other . . . This withdrawal, rather than going-out-to-meet the other, is an intense act of concentration, a model for which can be found in the Jewish mystical doctrine of Tsim-tsum. God as omnipresent and omnipotent was everywhere. He filled the universe with his Being. How then could the creation come about? . . . God had to create by withdrawal; He created the not-Him, the other, by self-concentration . . . On the human level, withdrawal of myself aids the other to come into being. (*Insearch,* p. 31)

But human withdrawal is a very painful and lonely process, because it forces us to face directly our own condition in all its beauty as well as misery. When we are not afraid to enter into our own center and to concentrate on the stirrings of our own soul, we come to know that being alive means being loved. This experience tells us that we can only love because we are born out of love, that we can only give because our life is a gift, and that we can only make others free because we are set free by Him whose heart is greater than ours. When we have found the anchor places for our lives in our own center, we can be free to let others enter into the space created for them and allow them to dance their own dance, sing their own song and speak their own language without fear. Then our presence is no longer threatening and demanding but inviting and liberating.

2. Hospitality and community

The minister who has come to terms with his own loneliness and is at home in his own house is a host who offers hospitality to his guests. He gives them a friendly space, where they may feel free to come and go, to be close and distant, to rest and to play, to talk and to be silent, to eat and to fast. The paradox indeed is that hospitality asks for the creation of an empty space where the guest can find his own soul.

Why is this a healing ministry? It is healing because it takes away the false illusion that wholeness can be given by one to another. It is healing because it does not take away the loneliness and the pain of another, but invites him to recognize his loneliness on a level where it can be shared. Many people in this life suffer because they are anxiously searching for the man or woman, the event or encounter, which will take their loneliness away. But when they enter a house with real hospitality they soon see that their own wounds must be understood not as sources of despair and bitterness, but as signs that they have to travel on in obedience to the calling sounds of their own wounds.

From this we get an idea of the kind of help a minister may offer. A minister is not a doctor whose primary task is to take away pain. Rather, he deepens the pain to a level where it can be shared. When someone comes with his loneliness to the minister, he can only expect that his loneliness will be understood and felt, so that he no longer has to run away from it but can accept it as an expression of his basic human condition. When a woman suffers the loss of her child, the minister is not called upon to comfort her by telling her that she still has two beautiful healthy children at home; he is challenged to help her realize that the death of her child reveals her own mortal condition, the same human condition which he and others share with her.

Perhaps the main task of the minister is to prevent people from suffering for the wrong reasons. Many people suffer because of the false supposition on which they have based their lives. That supposition is that there should be no fear or loneliness, no confusion or doubt. But these sufferings can only be dealt with creatively when they are understood as wounds integral to our human condition. Therefore ministry is a very confronting service. It does not allow people to live with illusions of immortality and wholeness. It keeps reminding others that they are mortal and broken, but also that with the recognition of this condition, liberation starts.

No minister can save anyone. He can only offer himself as a guide to fearful people. Yet, paradoxically, it is precisely in this guidance that the first signs of hope become visible. This is so because a shared pain is no longer paralyzing but mobilizing, when understood as a way to liberation. When we become aware that we do not have to escape our pains, but that we can mobilize them into a common search for life, those very pains are transformed from expressions of despair into signs of hope.

Through this common search, hospitality becomes community. Hospitality becomes community as it creates a unity based on the shared confession of our basic brokenness and on a shared hope. This hope in turn leads us far beyond the boundaries of human togetherness to Him who calls His people away from the land of slavery to the land of freedom. It belongs to the central insight of the Judaeo-Christian tradition, that it is the call of God which forms the people of God.

A Christian community is therefore a healing community not because wounds are cured and pains are alleviated, but because wounds and pains become openings or occasions for a new vision. Mutual confession then becomes a mutual deepening of hope, and sharing weakness becomes a reminder to one and all of the coming strength.

When loneliness is among the chief wounds of the minister, hospitality can convert that wound into a source of healing. Concentration prevents the minister from burdening others with his pain and allows him to accept his wounds as helpful teachers of his own and his neighbor's condition. Community arises where the sharing of pain takes place, not as a stifling form of self-complaint, but as a recognition of God's saving promises.

CONCLUSION

I started this chapter with the story of Rabbi Joshua ben Levi, who asked Elijah, "When will the Messiah come?" There is an important conclusion to this story. When Elijah had explained to him how he could find the Messiah sitting among the poor at the gates of the city, Rabbi Joshua ben Levi went to the Messiah and said to him:

"Peace unto you, my master and teacher."
The Messiah answered, "Peace unto you, son of Levi."

94

He asked, "When is the master coming?"

"Today," he answered.

Rabbi Yoshua returned to Elijah, who asked, "What did he tell you?"

"He indeed has deceived me, for he said 'Today I am coming' and he has not come."

Elijah said, "This is what he told you: 'Today if you would listen to His voice.'" (Psalm 95.7)

Even when we know that we are called to be wounded healers, it is still very difficult to acknowledge that healing has to take place today. Because we are living in days when our wounds have become all too visible. Our loneliness and isolation has become so much a part of our daily experience, that we cry out for a Liberator who will take us away from our misery and bring us justice and peace.

To announce, however, that the Liberator is sitting among the poor and that the wounds are signs of hope and that today is the day of liberation, is a step very few can take. But this is exactly the announcement of the wounded healer: "The master is coming—not tomorrow, but today, not next year, but this year, not after all our misery is passed, but in the middle of it, not in another place but right here where we are standing."

And with a challenging confrontation he says:

> O that today you would listen to his voice!
> Harden not your heart as at Meribah,
> as on that day at Massah in the desert
> when they tried me, though they saw
> my work. (Psalm 95.7–9)

If indeed we listen to the voice and believe that ministry is a sign of hope, because it makes visible the first rays of light of the coming Messiah, we can make ourselves and others understand that we already carry in us the source of our own search. Thus ministry can indeed be a witness to the living truth that the wound, which causes us to suffer now, will be revealed to us later as the place where God intimated his new creation.

CONCLUSION

A Forward Thrust

In the last chapter of this book I described hospitality as a central attitude of the minister who wants to make his own wounded condition available to others as a source of healing. Hopefully the implications of this attitude have become visible through the different guests for whom the minister is called to be a receptive host. Mr. Harrison, the old farmer, lost in the impersonal milieu of the hospital, afraid to die and afraid to live; the members of the inward, fatherless and convulsive generation; and those searching for new modes of immortality in the middle of a fragmented and dislocated existence—they are all asking for free space in which they can move without fear and discover new directions. When the imitation of Christ does not mean to live a life like Christ, but to live your life as authentically as Christ lived his, then there are many ways and forms in which a man can be a Christian. The minister is the one who can make this search for authenticity possible, not by standing on the side as a neutral screen or an impartial observer, but as an articulate witness of Christ, who puts his own search at the disposal of others. This hospitality requires that the minister know where he stands and whom he stands for, but it also requires that he allow others to enter his life, come close to him and ask him how their lives connect with his.

Nobody can predict where this will lead us, because every time a host allows himself to be influenced by his guest he takes a risk not knowing how they will affect his life. But it is exactly in common searches and shared risks that new ideas are born, that new visions reveal themselves and that new roads become visible.

We do not know where we will be two, ten or twenty years from now. What we can know, however, is that man suffers and that a sharing of suffering can make us move forward.

The minister is called to make this forward thrust credible to his many guests, so that they do not stay but have a growing desire to move on, in the conviction that the full liberation of man and his world is still to come.

THE TREASURY OF HENRI J. M. NOUWEN

AVAILABLE AT YOUR LOCAL BOOKSTORE OR YOU MAY USE THIS COUPON TO ORDER DIRECT.

ISBN	TITLE AND AUTHOR	PRICE	QTY.	TOTAL
17446-2	**The Genesee Diary** by Henri J. M. Nouwen *Report from a Trappist Monastery*	$9.95	x___ =	_____
00918-6	**Aging** by Henri J. M. Nouwen and Walter J. Gaffney *The Fulfillment of Life*	$9.95	x___ =	_____
18957-5	**Compassion** by Henri J. M. Nouwen, Donald P. McNeil, and Douglas A. Morrison *A Reflection on the Christian Life*	$9.95	x___ =	_____
12616-6	**Creative Ministry** by Henri J. M. Nouwen *A Spiritual Guide for Christians*	$9.95	x___ =	_____
23628-X	**Lifesigns** by Henri J. M. Nouwen *Intimacy, Fecundity, and Ecstasy* *in Christian Perspective*	$8.95	x___ =	_____
23682-4	**Reaching Out** by Henri J. M. Nouwen *The Three Movements of the* *Spiritual Life*	$9.95	x___ =	_____
41607-5	**The Road to Daybreak** by Henri J. M. Nouwen *A Spiritual Journey*	$11.00	x___ =	_____
14803-8	**The Wounded Healer** by Henri J. M. Nouwen *"Nouwen at his best"*	$7.95	x___ =	_____

SHIPPING AND HANDLING:
Parcel Post . . . . (add $2.50 per order; allow 4–6 weeks for delivery) _____
UPS . . . . (add $4.50 per order; allow 2–3 weeks for delivery) _____

TOTAL: _____

Please send me the titles I have indicated above. I am enclosing $ _____.
Send check or money order (no CODs or cash, please) payable to Doubleday
Consumer Services. Prices and availability are subject to change without notice.

Name:_____

Address:_____ Apt. #:_____

City:_____ State:_____ Zip:_____

Send completed coupon and payment to:
Doubleday Consumer Services, Dept. IM8
2451 South Wolf Road
Des Plaines, IL 60018

IMAGE

BOOKS OF
SPIRITUAL
NOURISHMENT

IM8 - 1/96